WRITING EXPERTISE

A RESEARCH-BASED APPROACH TO WRITING AND LEARNING ACROSS DISCIPLINES

T0018943

PRACTICES & POSSIBILITIES

Series Editors: Aimee McClure, Mike Palmquist, and Aleashia Walton
Series Associate Editor: Jagadish Paudel

The Practices & Possibilities Series addresses the full range of practices within the field of Writing Studies, including teaching, learning, research, and theory. From Richard E. Young's taxonomy of "small genres" to Patricia Freitag Ericsson's edited collection on sexual harassment in the academy to Jessie Borgman and Casey McArdle's considerations of teaching online, the books in this series explore issues and ideas of interest to writers, teachers, researchers, and theorists who share an interest in improving existing practices and exploring new possibilities. The series includes both original and republished books. Works in the series are organized topically.

The WAC Clearinghouse and University Press of Colorado are collaborating so that these books will be widely available through free digital distribution and low-cost print editions. The publishers and the series editors are committed to the principle that knowledge should freely circulate and have embraced the use of technology to support open access to scholarly work.

RECENT BOOKS IN THE SERIES

Michael J. Faris, Courtney S. Danforth, and Kyle D. Stedman (Eds.), *Amplifying Soundwriting Pedagogies: Integrating Sound into Rhetoric and Writing* (2022)

Crystal VanKooten and Victor Del Hierro (Eds.), *Methods and Methodologies for Research in Digital Writing and Rhetoric: Centering Positionality in Computers and Writing Scholarship, Volumes 1 and 2* (2022)

Heather M. Falconer, *Masking Inequality with Good Intentions: Systemic Bias, Counterspaces, and Discourse Acquisition in STEM Education* (2022)

Jessica Nastal, Mya Poe, and Christie Toth (Eds.), *Writing Placement in Two-Year Colleges: The Pursuit of Equity in Postsecondary Education* (2022)

Natalie M. Dorfeld (Ed.), *The Invisible Professor: The Precarious Lives of the New Faculty Majority* (2022)

Aimée Knight, *Community is the Way: Engaged Writing and Designing for Transformative Change* (2022)

Jennifer Clary-Lemon, Derek Mueller, and Kate Pantelides, *Try This: Research Methods for Writers* (2022)

Jessie Borgman and Casey McArdle (Eds.), *PARS in Practice: More Resources and Strategies for Online Writing Instructors* (2021)

Mary Ann Dellinger and D. Alexis Hart (Eds.), *ePortfolios@edu: What We Know, What We Don't Know, And Everything In-Between* (2020)

WRITING EXPERTISE
A RESEARCH-BASED APPROACH TO WRITING AND LEARNING ACROSS DISCIPLINES

By Linda Adler-Kassner and Elizabeth Wardle

The WAC Clearinghouse
wac.colostate.edu
Fort Collins, Colorado

University Press of Colorado
upcolorado.com
Denver, Colorado

The WAC Clearinghouse, Fort Collins, Colorado 80523

University Press of Colorado, Denver, Colorado 80202

ISBN 978-1-64215-170-1 (PDF) | 978-1-64215-171-8 (ePub) | 978-1-64642-393-4 (pbk.)

DOI 10.37514/PRA-B.2022.1701

Produced in the United States of America

Library of Congress Cataloging-in-Publication Data

Names: Adler-Kassner, Linda, author. | Wardle, Elizabeth (Elizabeth Ann), author.
Title: Writing expertise : a research-based approach to writing and learning across disciplines / By Linda Adler-Kassner and Elizabeth Wardle.
Description: Fort Collins : The WAC Clearinghouse ; Devnver, Colorado : University Press of Colorado, [2022] | Series: Practices & possibilities | Includes bibliographical references.
Identifiers: LCCN 2022059662 (print) | LCCN 2022059663 (ebook) | ISBN 9781646423934 (paperback) | ISBN 9781642151701 (adobe pdf) | ISBN 9781642151718 (epub)
Subjects: LCSH: English language—Rhetoric—Study and teaching (Higher) | Academic writing. | Language arts (Higher)—Correlation with content subjects.
Classification: LCC PE1404 .A348 2022 (print) | LCC PE1404 (ebook) | DDC 808/.0420711—dc23/ eng/20230210
LC record available at https://lccn.loc.gov/2022059662
LC ebook record available at https://lccn.loc.gov/2022059663

Copyeditors: Andrea Bennett and Don Donahue
Designer: Mike Palmquist
Cover Art: Nkosi Shanga. Used with permission.
Series Editors: Aimee McClure, Mike Palmquist, and Aleashia Walton
Series Associate Editor: Jagadish Paudel

The WAC Clearinghouse supports teachers of writing across the disciplines. Hosted by Colorado State University, it brings together scholarly journals and book series as well as resources for teachers who use writing in their courses. This book is available in digital formats for free download at wac.colostate.edu.

Founded in 1965, the University Press of Colorado is a nonprofit cooperative publishing enterprise supported, in part, by Adams State University, Colorado State University, Fort Lewis College, Metropolitan State University of Denver, University of Alaska Fairbanks, University of Colorado, University of Denver, University of Northern Colorado, University of Wyoming, Utah State University, and Western Colorado University. For more information, visit upcolorado.com.

Land Acknowledgment. The Colorado State University Land Acknowledgment can be found at https://landacknowledgment.colostate.edu.

Contents

WRITING EXPERTISE

A RESEARCH-BASED APPROACH TO WRITING AND LEARNING ACROSS DISCIPLINES

Introduction. What This Book Does and How to Use It

Why This Book?

The goal of this book is to introduce instructors from across fields to the idea that teaching writing and using writing for learning is everyone's responsibility—but that this responsibility is not an add-on or hardship. Writing is something we all do, and we write in the ways our fields require in order to get our work done. Everyone has learned to write over time, and the ways that we have learned are a result of where we have learned, how, who has taught us, and what has been rewarded by the audiences for whom we have written. Often our own learning as students and new professionals or instructors was through trial and error, and we did not necessarily realize we were learning to write and think in new ways as we became biologists or journalists, historians or engineers.

Regardless of how we learned, once we become experts at the work of our fields (academic disciplines, interdisciplines, or professions), our knowledge often moves from explicit to tacit. The term "tacit knowledge" refers to knowledge people forget they have and perhaps even forget how they learned it. Experts often don't consciously *know what they know* or think about it explicitly enough to explain it to someone else. This can make teaching difficult.

As we teach students and invite them into our work, we use language in the ways that our fields use it. We often don't realize that what we are asking students to do in an "essay" or "paper" or "proposal" reflects our own understanding of those ideas, which might be quite different from what students have done in other courses or settings. The work we do as professionals and scholars and the ideas we discuss and expand through our research and teaching all happen through very context-specific forms of language. The language and written conventions used by a biologist differ greatly from those used by an economist, dentist, or literary scholar. Teaching students to think, read, research, and practice requires inviting them into the written practices of our field.

Writing, then, is not separate from "content." It is a central part of everything we do. Yet we often don't know how to explain what we do to students. We are sometimes frustrated by the work students produce, without being able to explain what, exactly, is "not right." Their arguments might seem "off," their evidence might not be appropriate, the questions they try to answer might not be the ones we see as relevant or worthwhile. Students might use outside sources too frequently, or not frequently enough. They might not know how or why to reference other scholarship (and might not even know what counts as "scholarship").

Their terminology might feel "wrong," or they might use the words or phrases we expect, but in the wrong way.

This book is intended to help instructors surface what they already know about writing within their fields and to help them make their assumptions and practices explicit and visible so that they can better help students engage in them.

It is also a book that asks instructors to interrogate their values and practices to see whether they offer students and newcomers opportunities to bring their own experiences and perspectives and add to the conversations and change them—or whether there are rigid rules and conventions that (intentionally or unintentionally) serve gatekeeping functions.

Who Is the Book for and How Does It Work?

This book is intended to be used by instructors in higher education from across all fields. It can be used independently, in small groups by instructors from the same or different fields, or by faculty developers working with instructors on teaching using writing. Some of the book's activities are written to be worked on in pairs, though they also can be completed independently. This is an interactive working book. That is, each chapter describes ideas and overviews scholarship, but the primary work of the book is the interactive activities spread throughout each chapter.

The book moves back and forth between three, related ways that people use writing in teaching and learning:

1. *teaching with writing*, thinking about the ways that writing facilitates learning;
2. *teaching writing*, reflecting on ideas of "good writing" and how to help students develop it; and
3. *teaching writers*—facilitating the learning of those most important people, the students in our classrooms.

The book is intended to be used in sequence.

Chapter 1 asks you to delve into your field's work in order to identify your ways of thinking and practicing—your threshold concepts—and to consider where and why students typically find your field troublesome, or where they encounter learning bottlenecks.

With your field's threshold concepts in mind, Chapter 2 asks you to explore how writing works in your life and communities, and to interrogate common misconceptions about writing. Chapter 3 takes a deeper dive into writing, asking you to examine how knowledge is enacted through writing in your own field.

Chapter 4 then asks you to turn your attention to students and find out how your students experience your courses.

Chapter 5 considers how to put the ideas from the previous chapters into practice in order to structure rigorous and effective learning environments. In the appendix for each chapter you'll find examples of course and assignment and curriculum design from instructors across fields to illustrate the ideas from Chapters 1–5.[1] As you move through the book, we encourage you to keep a notebook (digital or paper) of all the activities in order to be able to refer back to previous reflections. You'll also find examples from other instructors woven throughout the text. In the digital editions of this book, they are linked; in the print version, you'll be referred to the book's web page or to other websites where the materials can be found.

Who Are the Authors?

We have both been teachers of writing in various forms for more than 60 combined years. We have taught first-year writing (aka "freshman comp"), upper division courses, and graduate courses; we've published many studies examining questions associated with writing, writers, and contexts for writing. We have also both been department chairs and administrators of various flavors in the universities where we have worked (public and private, of varying sizes). We both lead professional development events for faculty from across disciplines and across institutions.

Between us, we have worked with hundreds of instructors to think about writing and learning more broadly. We've listened closely as these colleagues have talked about their triumphs and struggles, about what they consider enjoyable and challenging about engaging with students as their ideas develop. As we've listened, taught our own courses, and conducted research about writing, learning, and cognition, we've developed our own faculty seminars and workshops. The framework for this book comes from our work with other faculty; many of the activities in the book are ones that we have used (or are modified from those), as well.

As we have written this book, we have thought a good deal about our positions as fellow instructors and faculty members, and as the authors of this book. Generally, we refer to readers as "you," though we just as easily could have used the collective "we." This is because this book comes from our own experiences as instructors who have learned to teach writing, teach with writing, and teach writers.

We are grateful to the faculty, graduate students, and undergraduate student colleagues from whom we've learned, and grateful to you as reader(s) for thinking about the ideas in this book. We hope that you will share your experiences and suggestions as users of the book so that we can continue to learn (and grow).

– Linda Adler-Kassner (ladler@ucsb.edu)

– Elizabeth Wardle (wardleea@miamioh.edu)

---

1. In addition to linking directly to resources on the web, we provide archived versions of the materials in the appendix on this book's web page at https://wac.colostate.edu /books/practice/expertise.

Chapter 1. Disciplinary Knowledge: Defining Ways of Thinking and Practicing

Writing is Never Just Writing

As instructors, it's likely that you see your job as teaching students something about your fields. These fields, though, are more than just labels that you and other instructors attach to a subject matter (history, biology, anthropology, law, business, journalism). Instead, fields are communities of intellectuals to which individual instructors feel that they belong, and to which they belong and contribute. Members of fields think through lenses that come from their own training *in* fields, because they have been educated (in graduate school or professions, in their lives as departmental citizens, and so on) to do so. This is why all instructors feel that their courses are intended in some ways to help students learn about, and learn within, fields. This is especially true of introductory courses because in those, instructors are likely trying to introduce key elements to potential majors. As students progress through courses, faculty ask them to do things with the knowledge they have been building. That "doing" includes ensuring that students can build on received knowledge, make connections between that knowledge and their identities and experiences, and even sometimes challenge the knowledge itself.

How people learn and make knowledge in fields or professions also shapes instructors' ideas about *writing* in those areas. That's because for *all* writers, writing serves three important purposes:

- First, writing helps people learn about and practice with how knowledge is made in a field. With writing, learners (or instructors) can find their ways into key ideas and learn to apply them; learners can also use writing to practice with how key ideas are intended to be presented in different types of writing in a field.
- Second, people can use writing to show what they know about those key ideas and connections between their understanding and those of others.
- Third, writing can help push the boundaries of how knowledge is created in their fields as writers bring in new ideas and even new ways of writing.

This book is about how you can teach writing in your courses and your field to help students do all of these things effectively. This book will help you work with writing and writers in research-supported ways in order to::

- teach with writing, so that students can learn about and practice with ideas;
- teach writing; so that students can demonstrate what they know in ways that your field expects; and

- teach writers, those students in your classroom, taking into account their ideas and experiences as you work with them to learn.

This book is also about how you can gain confidence regarding your teaching of writing and come to enjoy this work, seeing it not as separate from the "content" of your field but inextricably part of it and part of the expertise you already have.

To accomplish these goals, this book draws extensively on research in writing and learning. The primary focus will be on how you can study your discipline or field's knowledge-creating practices, then use writing to enable students to learn about and gain experience with those practices. We call this providing "access" to your discipline, because you are opening a portal into how the discipline or field works and the roles that writing plays in it. You'll also consider how you can create writing activities that learners can use to connect their own ideas and commitments to those knowledge-creating practices. We refer to this as providing "opportunity," because you are creating space for learners to push on knowledge-creating practices in ways that might broaden the discipline or field.

Access requires instructors to carefully study how knowledge is made (through writing), creating writing activities that help students study and practice these ways of creating. *Opportunity* requires instructors to learn what students know and bring to a course or a field, then do some reflecting on how students' ideas and commitments can build on (or even challenge) their own. These ideas of access and opportunity draw extensively on research focused on building equity that we encourage you to examine—work as foundational as that of Paolo Freire (1970), bell hooks (1994), and Gloria Ladson-Billings (2021), as well as researchers across fields who have added to their foundation of asset-based approaches such as Keivan Stassun (2011), Bryan Dewsbury (2019, 2020), Kevin Gannon (2020), and others.

This is not the only book that invites you to teach writing more effectively by analyzing expectations in your field or discipline. But it is the only book that places this examination within the context of access and opportunity, inviting you to sudy those expectations in the context of your own experience as a writer and learner and the boundaries of your field. It's also the only book that invites you to not only make these more explicit, but potentially expand your own ideas as a crucial part of equitable and socially just teaching. That's because writing is a mirror and a gate that (to adapt an idea from an important study in writing studies) "swings both ways"—writing is a process and a product that can exclude or invite students (as well as colleagues) and their ideas (Agnew & McLaughlin, 2001).

This is the power of writing: as a process and product, writing is the most obvious manifestation of work with and around creating knowledge, whether in an academic discipline, a workplace, or any other community where people share common beliefs. But it is never "just writing" (Adler-Kassner, 2017). Rather, it's also the primary way that ideas are represented. And we mean "writing" here in the most capacious way: composing that uses letters or numbers or visuals such as maps and charts, even composing that takes the form of code. All of these are forms of *composed knowledge*, representations of what people in particular fields or areas believe, know, and do. Those ways of knowing and representing are linked to what's valued, and what's valued represents the dominant knowledge of the field.

In this chapter, you'll start to outline the boundaries of your field, the dominant knowledge and practices of your field as *you* define them, the ones that identify how your ideas are distinct from other fields/interfields. You'll also start to connect practices within those boundaries to ideas about good writing.

Goals for this chapter include:

- defining the identity of your field
- starting to name central ideas (ways of thinking and practicing) in your field
- identifying places where multiple learners get stuck
- defining characteristics associated with "good writing"

Composing Knowledge

As an instructor, you are recognized as a person with the expertise needed to teach students. You also have the authority (and privilege) to do this teaching. But one of the characteristics of expertise is that experts tend to forget that how and what they do is learned and that expertise is demonstrated through continued engagement with shared characteristics and practices (Ambrose et al., 2010; Bransford et al., 2000; National Academies of Sciences, Engineering, and Medicine, 2018). Experts also approach all of their work from particular perspectives that reflect their experiences. Experts often see their jobs as teaching students to learn to cultivate the same abilities—the same expertise—that they themselves have. But as important as this idea of learning from and within field-based expertise is, it's often not something instructors think about explicitly because the whole structure of this learning is so familiar.

In this sense, a field or discipline is analogous to what is called a "community of practice." These communities are built and sustained by members who share ideas, language, strategies for learning, and markers of "insider" status (Wenger 1998, pp. 125–126). The trajectory from novice graduate student to expert full professor illustrates a person's journey into a community of practice—that person is learning how to speak, learn, and behave "successfully" in a discipline. Experts become good at these things—engaging and making knowledge together, knowing what knowledge is "insider" and what isn't, and how to demonstrate insider status. As these characteristics of expertise become more familiar, they become what people believe to be "commonsense." But as theorist Etienne Wenger reminds us, "common sense is only commonsensical because it is sense held in common" (Wenger, 1998, p. 47)—it's not "natural."

As a faculty expert, your expertise is reflected in your expectations for writing. This chapter asks you to take a step back and think about the context where that writing is situated—your own expertise and your (inter)disciplinary context(s). This reflects an important idea that writing scholars have explored and demonstrated through empirical research: *writing is a social activity whose value is determined and reinforced by audience(s)* (Bazerman, 2015; Lunsford, 2015a). This means that whenever any writer composes, they do so with certain things in mind: purposes for the writing, audiences who might read it (even if the audience is the writer), context(s) where the writing will be used. And when that writing is valued by one or more audiences, the very act of valuing reinforces what is manifested in the writing—the ideas, the form the writing has taken, and so on. Writing in any course, any program, in any field, is a social activity that is intended to speak to purposes and audiences (even if an audience of teachers) in a context that is valued by the people who reinforce ideas of "good writing."

Exploring Your Expertise

It will be useful to work on activities in this chapter with at least one colleague, though they also can be explored independently. If you are working with a colleague, try to find someone from a field very different from your own. You'll start your exploration by identifying as many differences between your fields as possible. By doing so, you'll engage in what researchers refer to as "experience of variation," i.e., conscious and explicit identification of differences across contexts (Baillie et al., 2013). (This is contrasted with "varied experience," the unconscious experiences that people often have moving from one context to another.) Engaging in conscious experience of variation—recognizing differences from one community of practice or context to another—can emulate the experience of novice learners. This, in turn, can help you think about what you need to make explicit to students about your disciplinary context and how you can help learners develop strategies to identify disciplinary boundaries. Asking instructors to identify *differences* is much more difficult than identifying areas of similarity or overlap, but challenge yourself to do so. Avoid the more "natural" pathway toward connection. Shortly, you'll see why noticing connections is easier for you than it is for your students.

Activity 1.1 begins the process by asking you to think about how you create your expert self.

Identifying Disciplinary Understanding (and Practice)

Activity 1.1 should help you to identify some of the most visible features associated with your identity as a member of a community of practice. But the boundaries of your field are considerably more complex. That's because (consistent with the "community of practice" theoretical framework) the labels, vocabulary, and understandings of learning within your field are manifestations of a deeper and more fundamental understanding of the field's *epistemologies*, or *ways of understanding*. Epistemologies are connected to ontologies, what people understand to be real (Roberts-Miller, 2019). Epistemologies and ontologies might seem to be a bit distanced from writing, but in fact they're integrally connected. Meaning is made within specific contexts, and shared understandings of meaning are created and reinforced when those doing and interpreting meaning-making activities (also known as "writers and readers") have the same epistemological perspectives and manifest them through practice—like the production of writing that a person perceives as "good."

On the flip side, when these epistemologies aren't shared, the perception is that meaning isn't being made. Instructors often express this mismatch by saying that a student's writing "doesn't make sense" or that what's being produced, often in writing, isn't "right." The question the writer is asking is perceived as being "off," or the evidence or data do not seem to be analyzed or incorporated correctly; the citational form seems not to follow the understood rules, or the language, style, syntax, or mechanics used feel inappropriate. But perceived inconsistencies are often the result of differences in epistemologies. Of course, not everything is relative; the point here is that many things that may feel like accepted "truth" or "common sense" are instead quite context- and value-specific. Thus, if you want to invite students into your field, you first have to make your disciplinary epistemologies explicit. Students can't access what they can't see or understand, and instructors can't teach students what they understand implicitly but struggle to make explicit.

Activity 1.1: Defining Your Expert Identity

1. How do you refer to yourself as a member of your field? (For instance: "I'm a historian," or "I am in composition and writing studies," or "I teach statistics.")
2. When you talk to someone not especially familiar with your field, what do you say that you teach students in your courses?
3. What are one or two terms that you use with colleagues in your field that you mutually understand, but that others are typically unfamiliar with? (For instance: rhetorical analysis, multivariate regression, null hypothesis.)

Two Approaches to Identify Disciplinary Epistemologies

As workshop leaders, we have found two approaches to identifying epistemologies that tend to resonate with faculty: the threshold concepts framework (Meyer & Land, 2003) and a method for identifying "learning bottlenecks" associated with decoding the disciplines (e.g., Middendorf & Pace, 2004; Middendorf &

Shopkow, 2017). Both provide possible lenses for identifying and naming what you know and do implicitly as an instructor whose identities are grounded in academic disciplines (or interdisciplines) or applied, practical fields. "Threshold concepts" help get to shared concepts that underscore participation in fields (including but not limited to ideas about what is "right" and "not right"); "learning bottlenecks" provides a way to think about where multiple students get stuck and to start unpacking why this is the case.

Threshold Concepts

Interviewing faculty at University of Durham, Jan H. F. Meyer and Ray Land recognized that in every field, there were particular ways of thinking and practice that students needed to understand in order to move into the work of the field. They called these "threshold concepts," ways of understanding that are specific to particular fields and which, once understood, influence what learners do. Meyer and Land describe the idea of "heat transfer" to illustrate a threshold concept: someone wants to cool down two identical cups of tea very quickly. They add milk to the first and wait a few minutes, then add an equal quantity of milk to the second a few minutes later. Which will be cooler? The answer is the second cup because "in the initial stages of cooling it is hotter than the first cup with the milk in it"; the steeper temperature gradient that leads to heat loss will mean faster cooling, even as the cold milk is poured into the first cup of tea (Meyer & Land, 2006, p. 4). Once home cooks grasp this concept, Meyer and Land say, it is "transformative"—they watch cooking shows differently, they choose pots and pans differently with the idea of heat transfer in mind, and so on.

The idea of threshold concepts has resonated with instructors and students in virtually every field. (There is an extensive literature on threshold concepts, a bi-annual threshold concepts conference, and seven edited collections focusing on threshold concepts theory/practice—see Mick Flanagan's excellent website for a range of examples at https://tinyurl.com/39v38vcj.) Faculty across fields have named threshold concepts like:

- Geographic and social environments dictate health behaviors and the consequences of those behaviors.
- Art historical writing involves multiple frames of interpretation and—perhaps more importantly—the ability to hold multiple frames in suspension at the same time while producing an original argument. While there is no one "right" interpretation of a work of art, there are interpretations and scholarly arguments that have more quality or staying power than others.
- Geography is literally and figuratively a worldview—exploring space, place, landscape, region, and environment—to better understand our changing planet, communicate that understanding, and apply it to decision-making.

- History consists of multiple and competing narratives.
- Musical works are produced by networks/communities of multiple actors with different things at stake.

Others are associated with actions, like this one that applies to a biology lab:

- Sterile technique is necessary because it ensures our cell cultures remain 'clean' and any experiments we do produce results just on the focal species.

To view more threshold concepts developed by faculty across disciplines, see the Disciplinary Writing Guides at Miami University's Howe Center for Writing Excellence, especially those from art history and philosophy at https://tinyurl. com/mwxaxy69. You can find also find archival versions of these guides on this book's web page at https://wac.colostate.edu/books/practice/expertise.

Scholars have identified seven features associated with threshold concepts:

- *Troublesomeness.* Threshold concepts can conflict with long-held knowledge, inert knowledge, and/or entrenched knowledge and practice.
- *Liminality.* Threshold concepts represent a "gateway" through which learners move. Meyer and Land write that a threshold concept is is a "portal, opening up a new and previously inaccessible way of thinking about something" (2006 p. 1), often (but not always) representing a change in thinking. For instance, the idea that "history consists of multiple and competing narratives" is a threshold concept; once learners step through the portal associated with this concept, they come to realize that historical narratives always reflect perspectives (and not objective "reality").
- *Recursivity.* Threshold concepts are not learned in a straightforward way, but rather in a "two steps forward, one step back" manner; the learning is ongoing and not always linear. This means that as learners move toward the portal associated with a threshold concept, they also wrestle with it.
- *Boundedness.* Threshold concepts specific to fields/disciplines. While there may be intersections between disciplinary concepts, there are also marked areas of distinction.
- *Irreversibility.* Once a learner begins to "see through" a threshold concept, it is challenging to reverse that shift.
- *Integrativeness.* Threshold concepts help learners make connections between what may have previously seemed to be unconnected ideas or phenomena.
- *Linked to expertise.* Once someone crosses through the liminal threshold of a threshold concept, it becomes increasingly challenging to remember that that concept (and epistemology) is not "natural" or "commonsensical," but linked to participation in a field (/community of practice).

For example, the idea that "writing is a social activity whose value is determined and reinforced by audience(s)" is a threshold concept of writing studies. This idea is so foundational for members of the field that to deny it—to assert, for instance, that writing is not social, or that its value is inherent only in its production—would mark a person as well outside the field; this belief has become a form of received knowledge. The idea is not arbitrary; it comes from years of research and theory about—and experience with—writing. This threshold concept reminds all of us that ideas about what makes writing "good" are reinforced by people in communities of practice, i.e., fields. (See Adler-Kassner & Wardle, 2015).

One way for insiders to start thinking about their field's threshold concepts is to identify what those concepts are *not*. Activity 1.2 asks you to take this perspective, and then Activity 1.3 asks you to flip your thinking to identify what is "missing" in the imagined discussion that 1.2 asks you to reconstruct. (Again, be sure to compile your activity notes in one notebook as you work through this book).

Activity 1.2: *That* Conversation

As you travel from place x to place y, the person in the seat next to you notices something you're writing or reading. "Oh!" they say. "That looks interesting. What do you do?" You place the text down and respond, "I'm a _____", or "I teach _____" (using some of the language you identified in activity 1.1).

The person then responds with an assumption about something you think, say, or do that isn't right at all, that in fact causes an almost visceral response in you. They say, "_____."

You respond to them, trying to reframe their thinking, "Actually, that's not quite right: I _____."

To illustrate, here are some of the ways that other faculty have completed this activity:

You: "I'm a mathematician."

Conversation partner: "I bet your checkbook is always balanced."

You: "Actually, math is about trying to find patterns in apparent randomness."

You: "I'm in writing studies, so I teach composition."

Conversation partner: "I'd better watch my grammar around you."

You: "Actually, we study what and who makes writing seem 'good' in different settings. We teach students to study that, too, then choose whether and how to write in those ways."

You: "I'm a historian."

Conversation partner: "I loved *Hamilton* because it really showed me the truth about what an important, liberatory figure he was for all Americans."

You: "Well, that's one interpretation of Hamilton—but it's just one. Actually, history is a set of multiple, sometimes competing, narratives about the past that can help us to try to understand historical actors/actions."

What the faculty are trying to explain in these illustrations starts to get at threshold concepts, because they speak to foundational ways of understanding, approaching, "seeing," and making meaning within their fields. Naming these foundations is key because they underscore so much of what's considered *good thinking*, and good thinking is one critical element of good writing. The examples you gave in Activity 1.2 gave hints about some of the threshold concepts of your field.

In Activity 1.3, you'll push this a bit further, focusing on concepts that are especially important for students who are just coming to your field. The grid found in Figure 1.1 can serve as a handy reminder of where to focus when thinking about teaching novices:

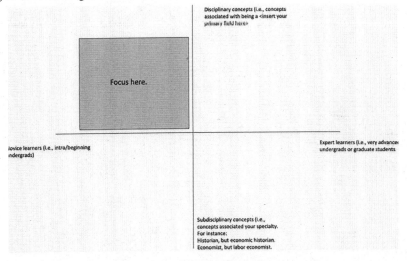

Figure 1.1. Where to focus when thinking about teaching novices.

Activity 1.3: Naming Threshold Concepts

Name one or two threshold concepts that you associate with your own field and explain why they are important for students in your course(s). One way to do this is to complete this sentence: "Sometimes, when students enter <this course>, they think it's about <an assumption students make about your field that isn't right>. But when they've really learned and explored the material, they leave thinking and acting differently. They put <this important concept or idea> into practice, which I can see when they <produce or do X or apply in this way>. Feel free to begin listing as many threshold concepts as you want to brainstorm.

Disciplinary concepts are ones that underscore the perspectives of instructors across the discipline, such as the idea that "writing is a social activity whose value is determined and reinforced by audience(s)." Subdisciplinary concepts are ones that are ones embraced by disciplinary subfields. For instance, for writing scholars with a subspecialty in technical writing, the idea that "technical communication simplifies complex information" is a subdisciplinary concept. Over time, threshold concepts must also be examined and expanded, too, so that they don't become reified knowledge that represents dominant thinking in a discipline or field (Wardle et al., 2020). For technical writers, the idea that "the translation of technical documents [and their interpreters] impacts the dynamic of . . . [translation] on specific communities" (Gonzales, 2022) expands the subdisciplinary concept; the idea that "writing only occurs within accessible conditions" (Womack, 2019, p. 26) challenges ideas of what is necessary for writing to occur.

If you can engage with other instructors from your own field during this brainstorming, so much the better. You'll find other examples of faculty who named threshold concepts and connected them to their experience of entering their academic fields in the appendix for this chapter (see https://tinyurl.com/2fhwj4je).[2] If you are interested in seeing whether people in your field have published about your threshold concepts, you can explore the clearinghouse created by Flanagan at https://tinyurl.com/39v38vcj. Once you've generated a list of possible threshold concepts, you can start identifying their implications for knowledge-making in your course(s). Specifically, you can focus on:

- what kinds of questions people in our field ask (what questions are "right" or "not right");
- what kinds of evidence or data is collected (what are the "right" and "not right" kinds of evidence or data);
- what methods should be used to evaluate what's collected ("right" and "not right" methods); and ultimately
- how what's learned should be represented ("right" and "not right" ways of writing about findings).

Chapters 2 and 3 will spend more time on each of these, but you can start making notes about your thinking now. You can also start comparing notes with someone in a field distant from your own. Sometimes the questions and methods people use seem like the kinds of questions and methods "everyone" uses. By comparing notes with someone from a different field and focusing on *differences* (not similarities), you might see that your way of thinking is distinct and specific to you and others like you.

---

2. In addition to linking directly to resources on the web, we provide archived versions of the materials in the appendix on this book's web page at https://wac.colostate.edu/books/practice/expertise.

In the appendix, you can find examples of how instructors from various fields have described their work, identified some of their field's threshold concepts, and considered the implications of those concepts for their teaching. For instance, a padlet created by Environmental Studies faculty member Summer Gray documents threshold concepts of that diverse interdisciplinary field for students in an upper division course, including "Infrastructure is more than physical systems; each system has a social and cultural life"; and "the design and construction of places ['the built environment'] reflect[s] social values and relationships" (see https://tinyurl.com/3uym8ddm). The padlet then links the concepts to case studies, activities in discussion sections, assignments and the final project. You can find other threshold concepts on the website for the Howe Writing Across the Curriculum Program at https://tinyurl.com/4s7m6fc8.

Faculty have created materials to walk students through threshold concepts, too. In a slide deck created by Professor erin Ninh for students in Asian American literature (see https://tinyurl.com/2p9japyr), Ninh defines "literary meaning" as a threshold concept: interrogating a passage "in pursuit of a research question and mak[ing] a case for your thesis/interpretation" by "see[ing] and fully persuad[ing] your reader of patterns of ideas that amplify or can even overturn the facile impressions of a first/surface reading." Then, she explains how to engage in this kind of reading, using the deck as a guide for her own teaching and students' learning. And you will see in examples from philosophy instructors Gaile Pohlhause, Elaine Miller, and Keith Fennen (see https://tinyurl.com/2s4yyrjj), efforts to help students understand how threshold concepts work in philosophy, particularly in their written texts. For example:

Threshold Concept: Transformative/Conceptual Reading

The statement: The goal of reading philosophical texts is to enter into different conceptual frameworks, by following lines of reasoning and allowing them to speak to us.

What this means for students: When reading a philosophical text, it is important to first try to understand the ideas and concepts being presented and how they make sense, instead of immediately reacting to them with criticism or judgment. Students should be open to the possibility that reading philosophical texts may activate new ways of thinking.

As another example, the Table 1.1 (excerpted from Loertscher et al., 2011), biochemistry faculty outline the threshold concept *steady state* and explain ideas that are "unlocked" for students once the threshold concept is understood, as well as connections that become visible to learners with a deep understanding of the concept. In this way, Loertscher and colleagues illustrate the ways in which threshold concepts are transformative and integrative.

Table 1.1. Threshold Concepts in Biochemistry

Name	Knowledge Statement	Biochemical ideas that are unlocked once this concept is understood	Connections that were invisible before deep understanding of the concept
Steady state	Living organisms constitute open systems, which constantly exchange matter and energy with their surroundings, yet net concentrations remain relatively constant over time. This dynamic, yet outwardly stable condition is referred to as a *steady state*.	Steady state is an emergent process that results from regulation of numerous biological reactions.	Once the condition of steady state is recognized, the purpose of complex regulatory systems in maintaining steady state and their connections to each other become apparent.
		Steady state is a metastable condition that can be maintained only because of constant input of energy from the environment.	
			Once the metastable nature of steady state is recognized, the importance of multi-tiered energy storage systems (starch, glycogen, triglycerides, etc.) becomes apparent.
	"Steady" is not synonymous with chemically "stable." Concentrations are determined by kinetic, rather than thermodynamic, factors. Hence, biological systems do not exist in a state of chemical equilibrium.		
		Steady state defines the conditions of life under which chemical reactions take place in cells and organisms. Therefore an understanding of steady state is necessary in order to correctly contextualize all of biochemistry.	

Name	Knowledge Statement	Biochemical ideas that are unlocked once this concept is understood	Connections that were invisible before deep understanding of the concept
	If an organism reaches chemical equilibrium, its life ceases. Consequently, organisms have evolved extensive regulatory systems for maintaining steady-state conditions.		

Source: Loertscher, J. (2011) Threshold concepts in biochemistry. Biochemistry and Molecular Biology Education, 39(1), 56–57.

Threshold concepts can be a useful lens through which instructors study their own disciplinary practices. For many instructors, the very idea of defining these concepts is transformative—as one faculty member put it, "threshold concepts are a threshold concept" (Adler-Kassner & Majewski, 2015). Since these concepts become lenses that instructors (or practitioners in any field) "see through and see with," they are integrally linked to ideas of what makes writing "good."

Decoding the Disciplines/Learning Bottlenecks

Some faculty find it difficult to identify threshold concepts without more extended thinking and conversation and prefer instead to identify "learning bottlenecks," an idea that comes from an approach called "decoding the disciplines" (or DtD). Joan Middendorf, David Pace, and Leah Shopkow, instructors at Indiana University, developed this approach after working with faculty teaching first year seminars there (Middendorf & Pace, 2004; Middendorf & Shopkow, 2018; Pace 2017). Middendorf and Pace (2004) realized that faculty frustrations over student learning could be understood to occur around these bottlenecks, places where students repeatedly got stuck. Studying these bottlenecks, the researchers and their faculty colleagues identified them as places where students were asked to participate in disciplinary concepts (ideas that also could be labeled threshold concepts) and knowledge-making in ways that were not knowledge in general but *particular to a field*. To work through these bottlenecks, Middendorf and Pace (2004) developed a recursive seven-step process for faculty to "decode the[ir] discipline for students." This process starts with defining those bottlenecks, then uncovering "mental tasks that experts [faculty] use to work through them" (https://decodingthedisciplines.org). Activity 1.4 works from the DtD perspective.

Activity 1.4: Identifying Learning Bottlenecks

Focusing on a single course that you teach, write ~100–300 words that describe a moment or conceptual action where the majority of your students seem to struggle, a place where things frequently don't go as you think that they should. As you write your description, be as specific as possible. The DtD website provides some examples of how to do this well:

English

Vague description of the bottleneck: Students cannot interpret texts.

More useful description of the bottleneck: Students struggle with textual interpretation. They want to "interpret[] without first getting a grasp of a text's content. They need to observe before they interpret...." (Ardizzonne et al., 2004a).

Biology

Vague description of bottleneck: Students have difficulty moving from fact learning to a deeper understanding of biological processes.

More useful description of the bottleneck: "Students have difficulty visualizing chromosomes, appreciating the distinction between similar and identical chromosomes (i.e., homologs and sister chromatids), and predicting their segregation patterns during mitosis and meiosis." (Zolan et al., 2004, p. 24)

1. In your written description of where your students struggle, circle the key terms or concepts associated with the bottleneck you've identified. In the illustration from English above, for instance, these might include *interpretation* and *observation*.
2. Write for yourself what you mean when you employ these terms. What does it mean to *interpret* a text? What about to *observe*? Literature faculty member Jim Kearney, for instance, often employs the metaphors of "text as artifact" (something to be observed) and "text as machine" (something that creates meaning that readers can interpret) (Adler-Kassner & Majewski, 2015, np).

As the examples in Activity 1.4 demonstrate, less helpful explanations do not take into account the ways that experts approach and understand key terms. More helpful explanations, on the other hand, take those terms apart and lay them out carefully—they "decode" the meanings that are implicit in disciplinary terminology. Instructors have also sometimes identified learning bottlenecks, as in the example of learning bottlenecks found in the appendix for this chapter (see https://tinyurl.com/2r9ha627). Shopkow (2010), one of the principal investigators of the DtD project, suggests that DtD can "facilitate the application" of threshold concepts for faculty, since it uses instructors' knowledge-making processes around those concepts as a "launching pad" to investigate how people solve learning bottlenecks and provides a "methodology [that includes] shared vocabulary of goals and techniques that can encourage institutional change needed to guide students through a process... while also providing the basis for fruitful conversation and collaboration among faculty" (p. 318). You can also find an extensive list of research using the DtD framework on their website (http://decodingthedisciplines.org/bibliography/).

Implications for Writing

Once you've started to identify threshold concepts or learning bottlenecks, you can start making connections to characteristics associated with "good writing." This is the focus of Chapter 2, but you can prepare for that chapter by studying the work of a successful learner in one of your own courses.

To complete Activity 1.5, you'll need to find a piece of student writing produced in one of your courses that you think is really good. You'll use this student work as the basis to describe characteristics associated with good student learning as they are manifested in that student's writing. *It really is critical that you use an actual piece of student work (that you can look at), rather than your memory of that work.* That's because grounding your analysis in text can provide you with much more concrete, specific, and usable evidence or data.

Activity 1.5: Describing Successful Writing

Begin by creating a three-column chart. Focus on a short excerpt from the piece of student learning that illustrates why you find it successful. (This could be one to three paragraphs of a piece of writing, a series of responses to a multiple choice test, or a particularly effective portion of a creative work.) Then, complete the chart below.

Describe: what makes this successful?	Reflect: What did the student need to know about and know how to do to create this piece of writing?	How does this writer's work reflect their acumen with a threshold concept or their ability to overcome a learning bottleneck?

Completing Activity 1.5 should help you to make connections across field-specific epistemologies, ontologies, and characteristics that you associate with good writing. Ideally, this will also help you to begin naming those connections so that you can share them with students. Activity 1.6 asks you to put those connections in "student-friendly" language.

Activity 1.6: Introducing Your Field to Students

Pick one course you teach that you see as central to introducing students to the knowledge of your field. Drawing on everything you have thought about in this chapter, write one paragraph addressed to students in that course in which you explain to them:

- The foundational element of disciplinary knowledge/threshold concept that you will focus on in this class.
- How those will be fostered through class structure, curriculum, assignments, activities, etc.
- How they will engage in both learning about and learning how (declarative and procedural knowledge) as they move through the course.

These activities should help you to start identifying elements of expert knowledge associated with "good writing," and then to make those elements explicit for your students, as in these syllabus excerpts:

Feminist Studies 20 (Laury Oaks and Catherine McGillveray) Introduction to Feminist Studies

This course offers an introduction to central concepts and issues in Feminist Studies, a department in the Division of Social Sciences at UCSB. Our readings explore the construction of gender and sexuality and the lives of diverse individuals and communities in the contemporary US within a global context. We will focus on the threshold concepts of gender, privilege and oppression, intersectionality, and feminist praxis. Students will learn how to understand these concepts within Feminist Studies, other fields, and outside the classroom.

Political Science 15 (Heather Stoll)—Introduction to Research in Political Science

This course is an introduction to research in political science. Its goal is to familiarize you with the social scientific study of politics. We will learn how to take a scientific approach to questions about political phenomena instead of the more familiar advocacy approach taken by politicians, interest groups, and lobbyists. In other words, we will learn how to ask empirical questions about the political world; how to answer these questions scientifically using the appropriate types of evidence; and how to clearly convey our arguments, evidence, and conclusions to others.

Access and Opportunity: Disciplinary Knowledge, Disciplinary Boundaries, and Inclusive Teaching

Activities in this chapter have focused on helping you identify elements of your expert knowledge, concepts, and practices. These underscore what you consider to be "good" writing and thinking. Forefronting these ideas helps create *access* for students in your courses. At the same time, Cathy Davidson (2019) argues tha,t when faculty work with students to learn in their fields, "We are passing on value systems as well as implicit bias" (p. 7). Threshold concepts reflect field-specific ideologies, cultures, identities, and experiences. In the United States, an examination of the constitution of academic fields shows that many of the faculty that have built those fields have identities that are read as primarily male and often white, unless one is focusing on a field that was constructed explicitly as a counter-narrative (such as Chicanx, Black, Asian, or feminist/gender studies). Most faculty have earned terminal degrees, and even those who do not have terminal degrees have demonstrated that they understand the field sufficiently to teach courses in it. Many faculty are also expected to contribute to research in the field, submitting to peer-reviewed conferences and publications. All of this work enacts and extends disciplinary knowledge, often through writing.

What happens when others with different values, ideologies, and ideas enter those communities? How can faculty consider the idea of field-specific boundaries *and* expand them to make room for others? One of the ways that people learn in any situation is to build connections between their prior knowledge and experiences as they enter new and different contexts. Your courses, especially at the introductory level, are intended to introduce learners to some of those elements of knowledge in your discipline or field.

That's why faculty need to foster *opportunity* in addition to access. Opportunity is created when we make room for others to bring their identities and experiences to a new community—maybe even pushing on boundaries based on those identities and experiences. Opportunity often means that faculty give something up to make room for others' ideas, too. The idea that faculty may need to do this can itself be a threshold concept. Making space for opportunity can be especially troublesome because of the disciplinary enculturation that all faculty experience.

We'll come back to these two terms, *access* and *opportunity*, frequently in this book. Providing both requires faculty to recall that *writing is a social activity whose value is determined and reinforced by audience(s),* starting to think about what's valued and what audiences faculty are thinking of (and reinforcing) in writing assignments. Faculty can ask: whose cultures and identities am I prioritizing here? Whose cultures and identities might be excluded? Taking time to consider these questions helps to make clear the choices that you are making when asking students to write, and considering these choices can be an important step toward building opportunity.

Conclusion

This chapter has introduced the idea that composed knowledge, aka writing, reflects epistemologies that circulate within courses and fields. It has suggested that these sites are communities of practice, sites where people learn to participate in particular languages, values, cultures, and strategies for learning how to learn. Before faculty can compose and teach writing in effective and inclusive ways, they must first examine their own disciplinary identities and start to make their assumptions about knowledge-making practices explicit, and then begin connecting those assumptions to their ideas about what makes writing "good." This is because writing is a social activity whose value is determined and reinforced by audiences; the things that make writing in one place or another "good" are determined to be so because the people who produce and use that writing have reinforced ideas about "goodness" associated with writing practices. These ideas about goodness are extensions of concepts that form "windows" bordering ideas about what is good and right within the community more broadly—the questions that are asked and not asked, the evidence or data collected or not, the ways of writing that are appropriate and not.

This chapter has also emphasized that faculty should identify and make the constituent elements of expertise (as they relate to writing) explicit, which is necessary for providing disciplinary *access* to students. These practices reify existing values of a field, and thus perpetuate existing biases. For this reason, making space for opportunity is also necessary if instructors want to invite students into their communities of practice. Faculty create disciplinary opportunity by intentionally designing ways for students to bring their identities, knowledges, and languages to courses and fields.

Chapter 2 will focus in greater detail on how you can begin the process of providing access by creating ways for students to study and practice with writing in your field. This study is an important first step for students to participate and challenge language practices, as well.

Preparing for Chapter 2

Activity 2.1: Writing Log

Before you begin Chapter 2, keep a *daily writing log*. For two days, start a two-column writing log. In column 1, record everything you write, large and small, formal and informal. In column 2, note purpose/audience for each piece of writing. You will use this log for various activities in Chapter 2.

Chapter 2. Representational Knowledge: Exploring Threshold Ideas about Writing

Conceptions matter. With our thoughts, we make our own worlds, to paraphrase Buddha. As Chapter 1 demonstrated, our ideas about what makes writing "good" (or "not good") are connected to our communities of practice. But the expansive connections between writing, communities, conceptions, and perceptions are sometimes reduced in practice to a set of *mis*conceptions about writing, and these are ensconced in popular culture through movies, books, legislation and policy, and behaviors of parents, teachers and friends. For instance, one common misconception is that there is one thing that constitutes "good writing." Another is "all good writing is clear and concise," with "clear and concise" being self-evident and independent of context. (For an excellent collection of "misconceptions" and their correctives, see Ball & Loewe, 2017). If we become teachers, these misconceptions can affect how we think about students and their writing, what we assign, and how we try to intervene (or not). What we do, and thus what we teach students about writing, in turn influences how students think about themselves as writers.

Most instructors from outside the field of writing studies have little if any training in how to use writing in their classrooms. They often hold the belief that writing should be taught by "English teachers" and that students should come into their classes—in anthropology, chemistry, engineering, architecture— already knowing "how to write." Though this also might feel like a common sense idea, it also is also a misconception. Chapter 1 introduced the idea that writing is a social activity whose value is determined and reinforced by audience(s); as people become experts they forget that their expertise has come from learning, is linked to their community of practice, and that what they know and do associated with that expertise (including writing) is not "natural." Research and our own experiences demonstrate that writing differs across contexts, how people write differs across disciplines, and learning to write well is a task that never ends. If writing differs across contexts and we are always continuing to learn as writers, as the introduction noted, then teaching writing is everyone's responsibility—but it is *not any one person's* responsibility.

Sometimes, accepting this more accurate understanding of how writing works can feel intimidating for instructors who don't study writing for a living. However, the task of including writing in disciplines and helping students learn to write (and learn *through* writing) is not as difficult as it might seem. You can tap into what you implicitly know how to do with writing in your field and add to that some of the research findings about writing and teaching in order to help students learn more and write more effectively in your classes, thus providing *access*. You also have the option of examining where beliefs about writing come from and considering whether and how you want to expand your ideas and practices, thus providing *opportunity*. You started this process in Chapter 1 through analysis of your own disciplinary knowledge—that is, through systematic reflection on your identity, expertise, and threshold concepts or learning bottlenecks in your discipline. You then started connecting this exploration to *representations* of field-based knowledge, connecting that knowledge to what you identify as "good student writing" and considering connections between these ideas and epistemological access and opportunity.

In this chapter and the next one, you will delve more deeply into how knowledge gets represented in writing. You will consider how to use these explorations to provide access to disciplinary and/or professional knowledge through writing.

This chapter asks you to use some threshold concepts about writing and test them against your own expertise, experiences, and knowledge, rather than simply accept them. Doing so will help you *teach writing*—that is, to more clearly identify your expectations of writing as they have been shaped by epistemologies of your field and make those explicit, then design activities for students to practice with those expectations. Both of these activities are a critical part of providing access, because you are creating ways for students to better understand and participate in your field.

Goals for this chapter include:

- gaining familiarity with threshold concepts of writing;
- undertaking systematic reflection on your experience of writing to test concepts against your own expertise, experience, and knowledge;
- using reflection to more clearly identify expectations of writing as they've been shaped by epistemologies of your discipline; and
- starting to make expectations associated with particular aspects of writing in your discipline more explicit.

The ideas you'll explore in this chapter build on the threshold concept in Chapter 1, *writing is a social activity whose value is determined and reinforced by audience(s)*. This chapter adds to that another threshold concept: *Writing is something people do, and also something that can be studied.* By studying writing, writers can understand more about how writing works; how people can learn to write; and how instructors can teach writing more effectively. This is good news for instructors who are frustrated by their students' writing but struggle to find ways to help students with the writing-related issues: There is research that can help! Through the activities in this chapter, you will explore how writing works in your own life, both personally and professionally, and then apply what you learn to your own teaching.

Threshold Concepts of Writing: Theory Informing Practice

Since writing is something people do that can be studied, this chapter introduces six research-based threshold concepts about writing. Then it asks you to study your own writing practices and history through these concepts, reflect on how these ideas work in your own writing practices and history, and apply them to teaching about and with writing in your courses.

Threshold Concept 1: Writing Mediates Activity Through Recognizable and Recurring Forms

Sometimes, people think that good writers reach into a "toolbox" and easily find just the right way of putting words together to achieve a purpose. But this is a misconception that ignores the complicated ways people actually go about composing. The writing log you created in Activity 2.1 as you prepared for this chapter (see the end of Chapter 1 if you missed it) likely illustrates this point: people write to accomplish various purposes—work through their feelings, share their research findings, remember what to buy at the store, ask for money. Writing "mediates" (or facilitates) these purposes (Russell, 1995, 2015). Your trips to the grocery are facilitated by lists; your research is made possible through funding, and the effort to gain that funding is mediated by grant proposals. You intuitively know not to write a grocery list like a grant proposal (and vice versa). You also know that writing for these different purposes looks different—a grocery list doesn't look like a thank you card, a thank you card looks different from an annual program assessment report. Different kinds of writing include different content and take different forms in order to achieve their purposes. This combination of content and form—different lengths, paragraph structures, sentences, fonts or modes of writing (e.g., on a computer versus by hand)—are *conventions* associated with these types (or genres) of writing. Conventions are formal or informal rules of writing, and they are reinforced as writing is used by people, for particular purposes, in contexts (Bawarshi & Reiff, 2010; Bazerman, 2015; Bazerman & Prior, 2003; Bazerman & Russell, 2003).

Conventions also have consequences. The more they are used and reinforced, the more they reflect the commitments and values of those who use and reinforce them. This leads to ideas about what conventions are "right" and "wrong" in any genre. These conventions, then, aren't carved in stone; they are created and perpetuated by users. For the audiences who make and use them (e.g., write and read written text, record and listen to or watch podcasts or films), genres and conventions are recognizable to users. So, too, are the ways that the genres mediate activities and reflect cultures and values associated with what is "good" and "works well." In other words: readers think a text is "good" (whether it's an academic paper or a novel) because it taps into what they believe that kind of text should look like and do—whether they think it should engage them in difficult and potentially troublesome thinking, or it should distract them from their concerns. If you want to share your thoughts with your local community, for instance, you know the options for doing that include op-ed pieces, billboard signs, letters to the editor, speeches at a town hall—and each of these has particular conventions that you can employ to best accomplish your purposes.

Activity 2.2: Purposes and Forms of Writing

Begin by making a list of the *purposes or goals* of the various kinds of writing you do in your professional life (e.g., record lab experiments and their variations, remember things, argue, etc.) You can look at your writing log to jog your memory.

Next, consider the *forms* writing takes when you are working to accomplish these purposes. (e.g., lab notebook, notecards, review essay).

Start with purposes and then consider forms. Often a single purpose can be enacted through multiple forms.

Purpose	Form(s)
Remember	Lists, notes
Share findings	Articles, letters, emails

Figure 2.1 shows some examples created by faculty in a workshop at Miami University:

Purpose/Goal (Why do you write?)	Form(s)
To share thoughts	
To preserve ideas and perspectives over time	Transcripts, records of hearing, client and conversation notes
To share outward manifestation of you	
To document terms of an agreement	Contract, letter of intent, email
To communicate data to shareholders	Annual report/financial report, regulatory filing, news release, journals and law books, periodicals
To establish/maintain precedent/to resolve issues	Judicial opinions (written statements), law review articles
To codify laws	U.S. code, state codes, local ordinances, U.S. constitution, administrative regulations
To support legal conclusions	Memos (internal and/or external), court filing, case notes
To explain concepts, provide examples	Textbooks, lecture notes, Canvas assignments, PowerPoints
To resolve problems	Arbitration awards, client discussions
To argue	
To inform/notify	summons
To persuade	Motions, journal articles, informal memos to clients, pleadings
To negotiate	Contracts, revised contracts (comments, underlining), mediation presentations
To criticize	Journal articles, op-eds

Figure 2.1. Left: list created by Martha Castaned, Darrel Davis, and Xiang Shen (Teacher Education and Educational Psychology). Right: list created by Chelsea Green, Karen Meyers, and Paul Becker (Business Law).

Before continuing with this chapter, consider the lists you've just made. What are some things you notice about *purposes, forms, and contexts?* For instance: perhaps that there are multiple ways to achieve purposes, and even the forms you list can look quite different depending on context.

Activity 2.2 asks you to put the concept that "writing mediates activity through recognizable and recurring forms" into practice by studying writing in your professional/academic life.

It's likely that the recognizable forms or genres you've just listed are extremely varied, that each purpose for which you write can be enacted through a variety of genres, and that the forms or genres themselves share discernible features and conventions but often vary in small or large ways. This practice of closely studying writing to show how forms you use often—forms that are, to you, "recognizable and recurring" because they are associated with your daily life and disciplinary practice and expertise—helps make clear what you know. Your understanding of these connections bring *implicit* or *tacit* knowledge associated with your experience (and likely your expertise) to light. The problem with implicit knowledge, though, is that people often don't recognize what they know. For instructors, this might mean that what you know about and do with writing in your personal and professional lives doesn't necessarily translate into what you assign to your students. Unfortunately, in school, writing is often taught as "psuedotransactional"—something that *pretends* to get things done (Petraglia, 1995).

Because the pressing reasons for using writing (in the case of students: asking parents for money, applying for internships, for example) are removed in psuedotransactional writing, the system of schooling tends to make up reasons for writing—to show knowledge on an exam, or in an "essay" or a "research paper" (forms that are created by teachers, in school, and are typically defined as whatever the teacher says that they are). They are "mutt genres" (Wardle, 2009). They're created only for school and they include rules that students often (rightly) see as idiosyncratic and unpredictable—a paper must have ten sources, or the thesis must come at the end of the first paragraph. Students often dutifully obey these, but without understanding why, apart from compliance with the rules of the assignment they are fulfilling. For instance, the writing portion of a standardized test like the SAT may state that it is an opportunity for students to demonstrate writing skills that they will use in college or beyond, but students are generally motivated to perform on the exam because their scores are tied to college admission. When the purposes are more remote—for instance, in written portions of state-mandated exams where they are asked to convince "someone" about an argument on a topic they know little about—students may be even less motivated to write them.

Alternatively, when writers (including students) see the need as pressing—an op-ed for a passionate cause, a research-based project that could lead to action on something that matters to them—they are much more motivated to write. Similarly, instructors who publish about their research have pressing reasons to do so. The conventions of the writing you produce for your research (no matter the form—writing, graphics, numbers, notes) are outlined for you—you know you have to use certain kinds of evidence, organize according to certain conventions, use certain citation styles. Research overwhelmingly shows that faculty *want* students to write for meaningful reasons (Eodice et al., 2017). It's useful, then, to identify why *you* want students to write and think about the connections between those motivations and how you support students' writing. Then you can talk with students about what they're doing, and how the genres and conventions they are learning mediate particular activities within your course (and community of practice). Some of the meaningful purposes you might consider, for instance, are to brainstorm, to engage with thinking, to identify intersections between concepts, to interpret facts, to connect concepts and lived experience, to apply concepts to real-world situations, to persuade others of something, to propose solutions. This makes the idea that "writing mediates activity through recognizable and recurring forms" visible for students, helping them achieve the purposes of writing that matter to you, your discipline, and your community of practice.

Helping students write for meaningful purposes will require bringing to conscious awareness what you already implicitly understand—that form follows function and writing gets things done—and asking yourself: what do I want students to learn and do? What forms/genres help accomplish those purposes? What are the conventions of those genres? How do I help students accomplish those purposes through these forms, and see this work as meaningful? Going back to the threshold concepts you identified in the preceding chapter can be helpful in this exercise. In the faculty examples found in the appendix for this chapter, you will see some ways that instructors have invited students to engage in meaningful purposes for writing.[3] Heeyoung Tai, a teaching professor in chemistry and biochemistry, invited her senior chemistry capstone students to write science fiction essays exploring ethical implications of scientific decisions (see https://tinyurl.com/4chacpxc). Bruce D'Arcus, associate professor of geography, asked students to contribute to a class website mapping the geography of COVID (see https://tinyurl.com/yckt89f8). You can also explore results from The Meaningful Writing Project at https://meaningfulwritingproject.net/ regarding what writing assignments students from different universities found to be meaningful.

Activity 2.3: Identifying and Supporting Students' Purposes for Writing

1. Brainstorm for three minutes: Why do you want students to write? What do you hope they accomplish? (Consider your own list from Activity 2.2 regarding your reasons for writing.)
2. What do they need to know, understand, or be able to do to accomplish these purposes?
3. How frequently and carefully do you provide opportunities for students to write for these purposes, and how much do you emphasize the purpose for writing rather than the form?

---

3. In addition to linking directly to resources on the web, we provide archived versions of the materials in the appendix on this book's web page at https://wac.colostate.edu/books/practice/expertise.

Threshold Concept 2: Writing is a Means of Learning and Creating New Knowledge

Writing is often seen as simply transcription of pre-existing thought: someone has an idea and they "put it down" or "write it up." However, this misconception misses the reality that "writing" isn't one thing—it's a series of acts that are imbued with different types of meaning, from using the act of composing to sort through difficult ideas, to putting ideas down "on paper" (or computer, or phone) for purposes from the poetic to the practical. It's rare that what anyone actually writes is exactly what was already in their mind. The act of writing is in and of itself an act of invention, of brainstorming, of learning, of working things out and exploring what we know and don't know (Bazerman & Prior, 2003).

For example, as you compose a grocery list, you remember items you didn't pick up last week, but you also remember that the grocery store recently moved its produce from one side of the store to the other and you start thinking about why that might be the case and what it means for sales. As you write the results section for a new article, you realize that you completely missed something about the data you had been analyzing, or that there are implications that you had not thought about before. You also use writing to process ideas—what you thought was straightforward actually requires more explanation. In other words, in the act of writing, you learn. As you learn and then continue writing, you create new knowledge. Writing out your results helps you understand them better, and then you publish an article that in turn moves forward a particular conversation in your field.

Activity 2.4 illustrates some of the many ways people use writing as a means of learning: making notes in margins, freewriting, sketching out big ideas and then rewriting them. All of these acts show that writing is much more than simply transcribing what you already know.

Activity 2.4: Tracking Thinking Through Writing

For this activity, you'll need to find something you've written for "academic" purposes (however you define that) relatively recently.

1. Identify a recent "academic" writing project in which you have engaged.
2. Write down everything that you can remember doing as you engaged in that piece of writing—from taking notes in the margins to emailing friends to making outlines and writing notes on a white board. Be sure to track your thinking and drafting from inception to final form.
3. Now step back and consider what you learned during this drafting process and how various kinds of informal writing helped you develop your thinking.

This threshold concept reminds us that the act of writing and learning is often quite messy. As writers think of new ideas, question old ones, run down rabbit holes, and try to sort out their thoughts, the written product itself is often messy, full of grammatical errors, and sometimes difficult for anyone but the writers (and sometimes even for the writer!) to read. That is a normal and even necessary part of the writing process.

School settings, on the other hand, can often ignore the fact that writing is messy. Outside of composition classes where students are asked to bring "drafts" of their work or to "journal" or "freewrite," writing is often simply assigned, collected, and assessed as a final product. When this happens, students miss the opportunity to see what they can learn and explore through the act of writing. It's possible for teachers to show students the ways that writing helps them (as teachers and instructors) learn, and to ask students to try out different methods for using writing to learn the course materials, explore their ideas, figure out what they know and don't know. This can happen through low-stakes, writing to learn activities (discussed further in Chapter 5) or by helping walk them through a higher-stakes, longer, or more formal project in ways that allow for time and opportunity to learn from the writing in messy ways before delivering a polished product for outside readers.

Assigning writing in this way again requires you as an instructor to reflect on what you implicitly know and do as an expert. If you assign students a research project, you can ask yourself how *you* engage with and learn as you conduct research projects. It's rare, for instance, that an expert would receive an assignment to write about an undefined "topic" using "ten sources" that is due in "six weeks." Rather, researchers consider pressing or troubling questions and often write about them in informal ways as they discuss them with colleagues over months or even years. Experts take notes as they read (and most likely not in the ways students were taught to take notes—if they were ever taught to take notes). They collect data and analyze it. They synthesize what they think they know in various messy drafts. Experts put ideas and findings together in all sorts of ways—sketching them out visually, putting post it notes across walls, writing outlines, writing pieces that don't yet make sense. All of this constitutes using writing as a means of learning, and none of it is typically visible to students or taught to them. Helping students engage with writing as an exciting and messy means of learning and creating new knowledge can lead you to rethink what writing you assign and how you talk to students about writing. How can our students know how to engage in long-term planning, note-taking, and messy drafting if they've never seen examples of this kind of process?

Threshold Concept 3: "Good Writing" is Dependent on the Situation, Audiences, and Uses for Which it is Composed

When instructors who study writing and the teaching of writing have "that" conversation (Activity 1.2) with new acquaintances, typical responses include: "Don't you find students' writing is worse than it used to be?" or "I better be careful that

I don't make any mistakes if I email you!" The responses reflect a number of misconceptions: that teachers of writing focus only on "grammar"; that there is one thing that constitutes "good writing" and that people either can produce it or can't; that everyone should have learned how to "write well" at some time in the past and that if they can't, it's because their former teachers didn't do a very good job teaching them; or that as students they didn't try hard to learn to "write well." These responses also suggest that people have been taught to believe that avoiding errors is the most important part of writing.

The more accurate conception of writing, however, is much more complicated. As you've probably seen thus far in this chapter, all writers are always writing something particular for a specific context and audience; none of us do—or can—"write in general" (Wardle, 2017). You write something specific for a particular purpose.

Activity 2.5: What Makes Your Writing "Good"?

Use the writing log you compiled to explore what makes writing good in your daily life. Pick three different kinds of writing from the log you kept. For each one, ask:

- Who was the audience?
- What was the purpose?
- What are appropriate forms/conventions for that type of writing?
- What makes this kind of writing "good" or "effective"?

Figure 2.2 shows is an example created by business law faculty members Chelsea Green, Karen Meyers, and Paul Becker during a workshop at Miami University.

Genre 1: Text message to friend	*Audience?* Friend
	Purpose? Sharing something of interest: an upcoming art show *Appropriate conventions?* Varies with person communicating, but: informal, maybe no salutation, more about the substance/content of message, maybe an emoji, sent quickly
	What makes it good/effective? Using casual conversation dialect/tone; conveying warmth, humor, friendly tone, build relationship, providing info they need, catching autocorrect
Genre 2: Judicial opinion	*Audience(s)?* General public (sometimes, broader), parties to a case, attorneys, judges, law students, political activists, NGO, private companies, government organizations, media, commentators
	Purpose? To resolve an issue, to explain a holding (the judge's holding in a case, "I find for the defendants etc. and here's why"), to set policy/precedent, to change and modify behavior, to facilitate planning
	Appropriate conventions? Formal: citations in body of paper (in blue book, the way lawyers cite things; to footnotes or bibliography); majority, dissenting opinions, and concurring opinions; sometimes one judge who writes it and others the court; everyone taking a position on the opinion; its own law language with law jargon and terminology used in particular context and framework that judges/attorneys understand but that general public doesn't; highly edited; "old-fashioned" prose; starts with who is delivering the opinion; includes some history and context;
	What makes it good/effective? Veracity of the arguments—should be analytical, not as "good" if heavy political opinions; conclusion should be at the end after evidence and analysis at the beginning, go through it objective, systematically, analytically; UNBIASED, based on precedent; flows, direction, theme, organized point to point, logic going one to another

Figure 2.2. Genre analysis.

As you've likely seen through this analysis, you make careful (even if unconscious) decisions about audience, purpose, and conventions all the time; these decisions, in turn, affect why and how the writing is "good" or "effective." The writing is "good" if it achieves your purposes and meets the needs and expectations of readers. For example, grocery lists are "good" if you get home in a reasonable amount of time with the groceries you need. Your text to your partner is "good" if they don't worry about you when you are late. There is no one monolithic "writing" and thus no one monolithic "good writing." Whether writing is "good" or not depends on the purpose(s) and the audience(s) for the writing. What is necessary is that the reader can understand without undue effort. Spelling or sentence construction in some instances doesn't matter until spelling choices or syntax are so unusual that they cause miscommunication. In the same way, the research report to your colleagues is "good" if it communicates findings and interests to your readers and convinces them of your viewpoint—or at least encourages them to ask questions and dialogue about the idea. Editors sometimes take care of the grammar and spelling edits, and what makes the report "good" is not that it is grammatically perfect or correct but that it is compelling and interesting to your colleagues. (One study, in fact, showed that readers adapted their expectations and critical focus based on their perception of who the writer was, looking for different things when they thought it was completed by a student, a colleague, and so on [Williams, 1981].)

The threshold concept that "good writing" is dependent on purpose, audience, and context may lead you to add more detail to the characteristics of "good student writing" that you described in Activity 1.5. On the website for Miami University's Howe Center for Writing Excellence, you can find a number of examples of guides written by faculty to explain what is expected of writing in their fields. Art historians Annie Dell'Aria, Jordan Fenton, and Pepper Stetler explain, for example:

> what is considered effective or good writing in our field varies by genre and purpose, but overall we expect to see:
> - a direct address of the subject or work of art.
> - an interpretive analysis of a work of art backed by research from credible sources.
> - engagement with significant interpretive and theoretical frameworks.
>
> See https://tinyurl.com/mrycm862.

Philosophers Gaile Pohlhause, Elaine Miller, and Keith Fennen explain:

> Our field tends to value precise thinking that considers potential objections and counter positions. Our relationship

to empirical facts is complicated, as almost all philosophers agree that there are no facts without an interpretive framework, and many philosophers are deeply interested in how these frameworks operate.

We tend to write argumentative essays and books. We rarely write reports or surveys.

We find writers to be credible when they situate themselves within a scholarly debate and when they use conceptual analysis, present a logically valid argument, and charitably consider opposing positions. Effective writing in our field tends to walk you through a sequence of thoughts about a question or problem, and may consider multiple sides, even those that the author disagrees with. Ultimately the goal is to draw you in and transform your thinking.

See https://tinyurl.com/2s4yyrjj.

Threshold Concept 4: Writing (and the Teaching of Writing) is Informed by Prior Experiences

Threshold concept 3 demonstrates that definitions of good writing vary. The next threshold concept pushes that idea further. If there is no monolithic "good writing"; if writing varies across genres, purposes, and disciplines; if writing enacts the values of the contexts in which it is used to mediate activity, then students come to classrooms enacting ideas about writing that may differ greatly from their instructors' ideas—because they have of course *had* experiences that are different from those instructors. (The realization that "We are not our students and our students are not us" is one frequently expressed by faculty who have engaged with the activities in this book; see Adler-Kassner & Majewski, 2015).

Prior knowledge and experience with writing can be challenging for learners and teachers in ways you might easily recognize. For example, students are taught to write in a literature class and this prior knowledge can present challenges when they need to write in a biology class. Or high schools students might have been taught to take notes in a particular way that is not effective in your course. Sometimes varied prior knowledge and experience is even more challenging, and can result in judgments about a person's home dialect that feel inequitable or biased. For example, research in writing studies, English education and linguistics have documented the challenges of valuing Standardized American English (SAE) over other dialects, especially African American English. This has led to efforts to teach "code switching" and subsequence concerns about this practice and its message to language users (Baker-Bell, 2020;

Conference on College Composition and Communication, 1974 and 2020; Linguistic Society of America, 2019; Smitherman, 1977). The use of specific language varieties is a complex issue, and you can learn more about it by delving into the sources cited in this chapter. The purpose of exploring this threshold concept is to help you recognize that all of our beliefs and decisions about language and correctness are informed by our prior experiences, cultures, idnetieis, and values. Reflecting on your ideas of what a really good learner/writer looks like can help you make your assumptions visible. You can then build these into assignments and class activities to strengthen and reinforce the characteristics of "good writing" you think important.

Examples in the appendix for this chapter illustrate how other faculty have answered these questions (see https://tinyurl.com/5y9z3ck6). Stefanie Tcharos, a music faculty member, writes that a successful learner in her "Exploring Voices" course was "incredibly open . . . to the unusual and unconventional subject and approach" and was "very willing to regularly participate and be engaged," as well as "very good at adapting the concepts and ideas to their own worlds." In more mundane ways, the successful learners in her course were "very organized" and "good about keeping up with their work." Rachael King, a faculty member in English, writes that in her course, good writers "show growth in understanding how to make an argument based on literary evidence. . . . This means making an argument that is about literature (rather than about the world, society, psychology) and that grounds that argument in specific, textual analysis."

Naming these characteristics may help you identify knowledge and skills that you can build into your assignments in order to help students be successful writers in your class and/or field. Instructors tend to expect that students can already write in the ways you want them to write because these ways of writing are familiar *for instructors*—that is, instructors bring their own prior experiences to these ways of writing. Additionally, because instructors are part of the communities of practice that value these ways of writing, the writing that you are concerned with is closely related to your expertise and the values associated with writing that are determined and reinforced as writing circulates among disciplines and fields. Instructors might think of these ways of writing as monolithic forms of "good writing"—especially when they have relatively limited exposure to writing in other disciplines. (When instructors do have that exposure, though, they sometimes find the writing of other fields to seem "jargony," because the language used is different from what they typically expect.) Sometimes, instructors also forget how difficult it may have been to work through the threshold concepts of your fields that are now common sense or implicit knowledge. Yet all of these assumptions mean it's easy to forget to a) find out what students' previous experience is with writing, research, and central ideas in your fields, and b) to provide some explanation or examples to help clarify your expectations.

Activity 2.6: Characteristics of a Really Good Learner/Writer

In as much specific detail as possible, describe what a "successful learner" looks like in a course you teach. If you can't focus on a learner you know personally, you can create a learner—the idea is to ground your response in a specific person. Ideally this person is real; if that's not possible, a composite real person is fine. After you describe a successful learner, consider the following questions:

1. How do you know this learner is/was successful? What did this learner think like, know, know how to do in their writing, etc.? (Please go beyond the grade that the learner earned.)
2. What attributes associated with the class might have or did the learner display—in class, in discussions with TAs or with you, or elsewhere?
3. What activities associated with the class might have or did the learner undertake—again, in class, in sections, with you, etc.?

Please include as much specific detail about what successful learning looks and sounds like in your description.

Threshold Concept 5: Learning to Write Effectively Requires Practice, Time, and Revision

Instructors often expect that students should already know how to write what they assign. This misconception, though, belies the reality that everyone is always learning—and everyone is also always learning *about writing*. In every new context, in every new genre, for every new audience and purpose, you must figure out something new. Whenever you take up a new topic or research question, the writing may be painful and prolonged even though you may have written "articles" many times before—each new task can be difficult and even painful. Every writer has to engage in the same writing task multiple times before it gets easier; every writer needs feedback and help from others; often writers fail and need time to fail and try again. No one is immune to the difficulties of writing.

Activity 2.7: Your Writing History

Freewrite and reflect for a few minutes on these questions:

> As a graduate student and then new faculty member, what kinds of writing did you have to do? What instruction did you receive? What was difficult for you? When you first tried to publish, what was the experience like? What writing project are you working on now? How difficult or easy is it? What help do you need?

In order to best help students with their writing processes and challenges, it can be productive to really think about and analyze how your own writing processes work. Given what you reflected on in Activity 2.7, are there areas where you can extrapolate from your own struggles in order to help your students? For example, if you were not given any instruction in high-stakes writing tasks and struggled for months or even years to learn, how could you help your own students have a different and more positive and more supported experience?

Activity 2.8 asks you to reflect on how you engage in writing you feel you do well and less well, thinking through how your process works and who helps with it.

Activity 2.8: Your Writing Processes

For this activity, reflect on something you've written professionally that you are used to writing and feel you do fairly well:

1. What sorts of planning, feedback, and revision do you need to write this type of text effectively? How many drafts? How long is the planning period?
2. What sorts of readers help you revise and generate ideas?
3. Who is your "ideal" reader for a rough draft? What are the characteristics of an effective reader of your work?
4. When in the drafting/invention process do you get feedback and talk things over with others?

After you respond to these questions, answer them a second time while focusing on a less familiar type of writing or for a more challenging context (a journal where you haven't published before or a new kind of report or proposal or even a syllabus for a new class). How are your responses different?

Activities 2. 7 and 2.8 are intended to help you bring to conscious awareness some of the challenges of writing. Instructors' familiarity with school settings might make it easy to forget just how difficult writing can be, how much time it can take, how much help and revision writers tend to need. To resist this, it is helpful to reflect on what writing is like for you—and what writing was like for you before you got good at a particular genre or way of writing.

Activity 2.9 asks you to focus even more narrowly on a time when things didn't go as planned with writing. Reflecting on these moments can be important for thinking about what kind of support works best for you— and thus what might also support your students.

When you seek to build support and scaffolding for your students, it is especially important to remember when your efforts to write haven't gone as you planned— maybe even times when your efforts resulted in what you saw as failure. Remembering your own struggles as a writer can help you gain empathy for students (a subject taken up in Chapter 4). Everyone has been a learner, and everyone is still learning. Learners often fail before they succeed. Remembering these writing experiences is important in building scaffolded writing opportunities for your students.

Activity 2.9: A Time You Did Not Succeed When Writing

Think of a time you "failed" when attempting to write about something new or for a new field or in a new form or for a new audience. Then, write about the following questions:

1. How long did it take before you were able to write in expected ways?
2. What happened? How did you finally succeed (if you did)? What helped you?

Threshold Concept 6: Writing Enacts and Creates Disciplinary Identities and Values

In writing faculty development workshops, faculty often ask why students can't write in the ways that the instructor expects them to. The irony is that instructors in varied fields all expect something different—without explicitly recognizing this reality. The common assumption is that there is one kind of "academic writing" from which all other writing stems, and that all instructors agree on what that might be. This is not the case, however (Russell 1995).

Although genres can have similarities across related disciplines (e.g., biology and psychopharmacology) (Carter, 2007), there are many more ways in which genres and conventions vary, both subtly and dramatically. This goes back to the idea that writing enacts and (re)creates the values and identities of fields. As writers learn to compose in the ways colleagues write, they begin to embody the voices, values, and identities of the communities where the writing circulates (and is validated). And, over time, those ways of composing become invisible to them; they start to feel like "conventions in general"—thus the conventions and the values they embody start to become invisible the longer a writer uses them. For example, as someone writing in STEM disciplines uses passive voice and avoids first person in professional articles and reports, they are embodying the belief that scientific knowledge is objective; this may not be a conscious act, however, just what is expected of them by the people with whom their writing is in dialogue. As someone writing in history weighs varying accounts of historical events, they enact the value and threshold concept that history consists of multiple and competing narratives and there is no single, objective, capital-T Truth. If someone in education cites dozens of other scholars before stating their own argument, they illustrate the value of giving "due regard" to colleagues (Hyland, 2013, p. 13).

You may chafe at the request to reflect on the conventions of writing (and values) that your field asks you to use. After all, these values and conventions were created by others and expected of you, and may not reflect your personal beliefs or values. They may have solidified as expectations decades ago and may not align well with current field members' research or with the available technologies. At times, we may determine that the values and conventions of a particular discipline are so different from our own that we do not wish to remain in the field. At other times, we might help change the conventions and values. As values and activities of fields change, so too does the writing—sometimes the changes happen quickly, other times they happen slowly. As written values and conventions change, so, in turn, does the field. Reflecting on this connection between values and ways of writing is yet another way to observe how *opportunity* has contributed to the field—that is, how making room for other values, ideas, and commitments has led the field's boundaries to change (or, in some instances, has not led to change—and instead resulted in people leaving the field).

The conscious experience of learning to write like other members of your field may quickly fade from memory as you become more successful in that field. By the time you become an expert, designing classes for students to learn about the field, you know "good" writing from your field when we see it. But you may not have the language to talk about what writers must do in order to create that good writing, or why these particular conventions are considered good. Part of helping students understand your written disciplinary conventions and values involves bringing them to your own conscious awareness and naming them for others.

Activity 2.10: Learning and Using Your Field's Written Conventions

1. Without referencing a text, write down all of the "rules" you keep in mind when you are composing a research-based piece of writing (article, paper, or book) for colleagues in the discipline. (For instance: always start with a narrative, never use first person, shorter is better, never cite year but always cite person).
2. Pick a few of these that tripped you up when you began writing in your discipline/profession.
3. How did you learn to enact these values and conventions? Who helped you? What got in your way?

Bringing these conventions and expectations to conscious awareness and sharing them with students can go a long way toward making writing in your field accessible and learnable for your students. It's also worth remembering that there's an important power dynamic at work in this relationship, too. Consider, for instance, what it would be like to write a short note to a former teacher or advisor of yours telling them what kind of support you would like to have received in order to better introduce you to the idiosyncrasies of writing in your field when you were a student yourself. Does this idea seem acceptable? Outrageous? Something that would be welcomed, or would never be done? Answering these questions helps make clear some of the ways that members of your field show how knowledge is made—and as a reminder, making those knowledge-creating practices visible to students is a key part of facilitating access.

Activity 2.11: Building a Supportive Writing Process for Your Students

Identify an assignment you give your students that you also regularly write (a "research paper" or "lab report" or "grant proposal" for example).

1. What steps, supports, opportunities for peer interaction, and feedback do *you* need in order to write this kind of text?
2. How might you revise the assignment to better support your students in their efforts to write this same text? What do they need to know in order to begin? What invisible steps and abilities and supports need to be made visible? How much time will students need to engage in the process as you do?

Conclusion

This chapter has introduced some misconceptions about writing and worked to counter them with research-based threshold concepts about writing that inform the ways in which writing is used and taught in fields:

- writing mediates activities through recognizable and recurring forms
- writing is a means of learning and creating new knowledge
- definitions of "good writing" depend on the situation, audiences, and uses for which writing is composed
- writing is informed by prior experience
- learning to write effectively requires practice, time, and revision
- writing enacts and creates disciplinary identities and values

These ideas can become a very powerful foundation for creating access and opportunity for your students. When you recognize that writing is something that is created and which circulates within communities of practice for particular purposes and that those creations and purposes both perpetuate the communities and beliefs about what is "important" in them, you can then more easily explain to students why writing looks the way(s) that it does. Suddenly, ideas that once might have seemed arbitrary and strangely idiosyncratic make more sense. At the same time, the ideas that you've started to explore here also serve as a reminder that all writers come to your courses with varied ideas about what's expected, and these ideas are formed by their prior experiences in school and outside. This reality can help you remember to build in practice, time, and revision (with feedback)—because we are all always learning to write. The next chapter will invite you to dive more deeply into how disciplinary knowledge is represented in writing as a way to open *access to your courses.*

Preparing for Chapter 3

For most of the activities in the next chapter, it will be helpful to find a partner from a field dissimilar from yours. You also will want to find a research article from your field that you will share with that partner for some of the activities in Chapter 3.

Chapter 3. Disciplinary Discourse: Examining How Disciplinary Knowledge is Represented

Chapter 2 described in greater detail how some of writing's threshold concepts can inform your approach to teaching writing. You also started to consider how writing works in your field. These ideas should provide greater insight into a central assertion of this book: "good writing" is shaped by contexts, the places where the writing is being done; the writer's purpose, which is informed by their identities; and audiences, the people for whom the writing is being created.

How people produce this writing is influenced by their prior experiences as writers and by how understandings of writing have been conveyeds. Sometimes, this has been in school, through different assignments to teaching and grading; often, it has been out of school. The threshold concepts identified in Chapters 1 and 2 provided activities for you to explore the assertion that "good writing" is shaped by contexts, audiences, and purposes, as well as activities for you to act on it: naming your disciplinary threshold concepts; considering the values, conventions, and goals of your disciplinary work; analyzing the nature of writing and how writing works in your field.

Where Chapter 2 focused on this idea from a 10,000-foot perspective, this chapter asks you to zoom in and spend some time closer to the ground. Here, you'll conduct an analysis of specific elements of writing in your field and explore: what kinds of questions do people in your field ask? What kind of evidence or data do they collect and expect? What methods do they use to interpret or analyze that evidence? How are the results of that work conveyed *in writing*? How are their citations field-specific? Considering these questions will help you teach writing because you'll start to pay close attention to these aspects of writing that most people take for granted, the ones that seem immutable and incontrovertible. As this book has already suggested, one field's idea of what can and must be done in writing can sometimes be in direct conflict with the imperatives of other fields, and what one faculty member considers the correct and only way to write, another would find absolutely incorrect.

Goals for this chapter include:

- helping you closely study elements of writing that you often take for granted or that seem "invisible";
- bringing your disciplinary conventions to conscious awareness;
- studying research writing and citational practice in your field;
- gaining some language for talking about linguistic conventions and rhetorical "moves"; and

- developing language to talk with students about elements of writing (especially research-based writing) that you and they might take for granted).

As you undertake the activities in this chapter, you will be asked to "translate" your analysis (Gonzales, 2018) into language you might use with students. That's because research shows that talking about how fields work (and, in this instance, how the genres of those fields work) may result in a number of important outcomes: mitigating stereotype threat, decreasing distance between student and instructor, and cluing students in to "how things work in this place" (Harrison et al., 2019; Seidel et al., 2015).

How Written Genres and Writers Reflect the Values of Fields

Chapter 2 introduced the idea that while the conventions of types of writing might seem obvious, rigid, and even like "common sense" to you, they are instead specific characteristics of *genres* of writing that circulate within communities of practice. In everyday practice, the term "genre" is often understood to mean "category." For instance, playlists are sorted into genres like R&B, country, rap, classic rock; literature is sorted by categories such as fiction, mystery, science fiction, romance, or nonfiction. But researchers who study written discourse have demonstrated that genres are more than simply categories. People produce genres in response to rhetorical situations that they encounter regularly, and they use genres to achieve their purposes. Chapters 1 and 2 also introduced the idea that these characteristics are produced within communities of practice, including academic disciplines. The threshold concepts in Chapters 1 and 2 also demonstrated how writing in disciplinary genres mediates activities. Writing does this mediational work through recognizable and recurring genres—and in academia, these are most often the genres of the fields (Bazerman, 2015; Hart-Davidson, 2015).

Within those communities of practice, ideas of what "good writing" looks like play important roles. As they are used by people in the communities, they become accepted as "correct" or even "the right way to write." Researchers studying communication thus say that genres *enact* values, conventions, priorities, beliefs, and even power structures of the communities where they are used.

In this context, *enact* means both "use" and "perpetuate," because each time the genres are used they recreate and reinforce beliefs and values about 'correctness' by their users. It is critical to understand not only what is defined as "correct" within genres, but also the values that these ideas of "rightness" reinforce in order to create *access* for disciplinary novices. Once people have learned textual conventions of disciplinary genres and use them regularly, the conventions seem obvious, perhaps even like "genres-in-general" (Wardle, 2009)—just "how things are." Thus, it may be difficult for experts to even name the conventions they use and expect their students to use. Experts may not see genres and genre conventions as something that needs to be named, they may not consciously see the conventions at all, or they may no longer have the language for talking about them. However, naming and providing ways for students to practice with the conventions of these genres—with the ideas (content) of writing *and* the way that those ideas are presented as an argument or thesis or main idea, supported with evidence from others, cited, and shaped in written form—is a critical part of providing disciplinary access. That's because written genres (both their content and their conventional forms) reflect the ways in which people join or belong to fields, and perpetuates the ideas circulating within those fields (Lerner, 2015).

Disciplinary Genres

When students are asked to write in new genres—or in known genres but in a new field or other context—they are being asked to enact a new set of values associated with the genre. To do this well, they benefit from looking at examples of what is expected and considering what is constant, what changes, and how writers use language to achieve the goals of the genre. The next two activities guide you through analysis of a genre in your field—first, a broad overview that you'll do with a partner (Activity 3.1), and then a close analysis (Activity 3.2) that you'll conduct on your own.

This activity of analyzing examples of one genre is a useful one to share with your students when you assign something that may be new to them. You can teach them to collect examples in order to look for patterns across them, but you must also serve as a sort of "insider informant" who helps them understand why the genre exists, who and what it does, and why.

While this sort of genre analysis is useful with any new genre students are asked to write, the rest of this chapter will explicitly focus on research genres as one "site" for thinking about how values, conventions, and goals of various fields are enacted in texts.

Activity 3.1: Trying to Understand an Unfamiliar Genre

For this activity, pick several examples of one genre that is fairly common in your field but that you think your partner may not be familiar with (for example, a musical score, an artist's statement, a poster presentation, notes on a piece of software code, etc.). Be sure to collect several examples of this one genre so that your partner can look across the examples in order to try to see patterns.

Trade examples with your partner but do not provide them with any contextual information. As you look at your examples of one genre that your partner brought, try to determine the answers to these questions (modified from Sonja Foss' (1989) excellent text *Rhetorical Criticism*):

1. What is the genre? Can you name it?
2. When and why do you think people compose this genre?

3. As you look across the examples of the genre, what content does it typically contain? What contents seem optional or variable?
4. What is the genre intended to do? What activity is it mediating? How can you tell?
5. How is the genre typically organized? What comes first, next, after that? Does the organization vary across the examples of the genre?
6. What seems to make this genre what it is? (What elements must be there for it to be what it is)?

After individually examining the examples of the genres you each brought, trade responses. How well have you figured out the genre your partner brought, and vice versa? What were you able to figure out from asking these questions, and what weren't you able to figure out?

Finally, share with your partner what you might need from them if you were a student being asked to write this genre for the first time. What seems hardest for you? What might you need the most help with? What seems particularly strange to you?

Activity 3.2: Rhetorical Scan of Research Writing from Outside Your Field

Trade research articles with your partner. Initially, do not share any context or information. Instead, do a quick rhetorical scan. As you do the following things, take notes that you can then share with your partner.

1. Skim the article from the other field from beginning to end, focusing on the pages, layout, sections, citations, visuals, footnotes, etc.—not the content. You don't want to read it closely now.
2. What seems familiar to you?
3. What seems strange or unfamiliar or unexpected? (Be sure to consider things like citation style, use of headings or footnotes, visuals, length, number of citations, length of paragraphs, etc.).

Share your reflections with your partner. Where are you seeing similarities and differences across your text and theirs?

The Elements of Effective Research Genres Within and Across Fields

The purpose of many academic genres is to share research findings and engage in the scholarly conversations of the field through inquiry. All of this work is mediated by the social institutions in which it occurs (universities, labs, and so on) and the disciplinary communities of practice that determine what "counts" and what doesn't. Research writing in the academy happens within and for different academic contexts and thus differs in many ways across fields. However, instructors often imagine and talk about academic writing as monolithic, telling their students to produce "good academic writing." While it is certainly possible to identify some conventions of writing that span across fields, as noted in the previous chapter, students tend not to see these similarities (McCarthy, 1987). In fact, in many cases, the differences are quite complicated in both obvious ways (some fields embrace first person and others never allow it; some use APA and others use MLA for citation) and quite subtle ways (different appeals to background knowledge, different means of establishing "truth"). Experts may use disciplinary citational forms as a shorthand to summarize all of the conventions they want students to use: "Write an APA paper," or "Write an MLA paper." However, these shorthands gloss over multiple conventions that novices have not yet learned. Experts immersed in disciplinary ways of thinking and practicing are often unable to recognize what they do as specialized and particular, and instead mistake their rhetorical moves for what David Russell (1995) calls universal educated discourse.

Helping students learn to write in your field first requires you to recognize that what you recognize as "good" academic writing is often unique to your own field (and maybe adjacent ones); once you recognize what is unique about how *you* write, you can, in turn, help students understand and practice with the conventions of that writing. Activities 3.2 through 3.5 ask you to look at a research article from outside your own field and examine elements that might be strange to you. Doing this reflective comparison should help you be better able to see and name the elements of writing in your field that may previously have been invisible to you.

For these activities you will again want to try to work with a partner, preferably one from a field as different from yours as possible. Each of you should select a research article/paper that you feel reflects the expectations for conveying knowledge (however you define that) in your field. Be sure to choose a *research article* for this activity, rather than another scholarly genre such as a book review.

There are specific ways that academic research genres can vary—multiple places where differences can be readily analyzed, including introductions to research-based writing, and the ways that authors work to make these texts convincing to readers. You will consider these next.

Research Introductions

The first place where research articles can vary is in their introductions. While all introductions share some common elements, or what linguist John Swales (1990) calls rhetorical "moves," the ways the moves are enacted differ quite a bit from one field to the next. Understanding and naming what these "moves" are and how they vary can be quite helpful for students because it helps them see how there are common features of "academic writing," but different fields enact those features in different ways that embody the values and goals of their work.

Rhetorical Move 1: Establish a territory.

"Establishing a territory" refers to the ways that writers situate their research within the field and acknowledge their awareness of related work. Writers can establish a territory by:

- claiming centrality ("recently there has been a spate of interest in . . ." or "knowledge about Y is important for . . .") and/or
- making topic generalizations ("the properties of X are not well understood . . ." or "X is a common finding in patients with . . .") and/or
- reviewing previous research.

Rhetorical Move 2: Establish a niche.

"Establishing a niche" refers to the ways writers demonstrate a need for their own contributions as they're related to the field and the territory they've established. Writers establish a niche by:

- counter-claiming ("Jones and Riley believe X, but . . .");
- indicating a gap ("While existing studies do Y, they have not . . .");
- question-raising ("While Jones and Riley have established X, a number of questions remain . . ."); and/or
- continuing a tradition ("Earlier studies suggest . . . and more work is needed").

Rhetorical Move 3: Occupy the niche.

"Occupying the niche" refers to the ways that writers assert how their research contributes to existing knowledge and how they will go about demonstrating their claims. Writers occupy the niche they have established by:

- outlining purposes,
- announcing present research,
- announcing principle findings, and
- indicating the structure of the research article.

Recognizing how researchers in your field establish the territory, identify the niche, and then occupy that niche can help you identify how these common moves look in *your field*.

As you consider the similarities and differences in how the articles from your two fields work to set up and establish a space for research, consider the challenges for students in producing "research papers" as they write across their general education, elective, and majors courses. Without examples and directions, it may be difficult for them to know what is expected, even in what may feel like the simplest elements of introducing and framing their ideas.

Activity 3.3: The Moves of a Research Introduction

Look again at the research article that your partner has shared with you. Try to identify the introduction and beginning of the article (up to the point where the methods or analysis or beginning of the writer's own research begins). Note that in some fields this is clearly marked, while in others, it is not.

1. Identify where and how each of the three moves are made:
    a. establishing a territory,
    b. establishing a niche, and
    c. occupying the niche.

    Be sure to highlight words or phrases that cue you that the writer is making these moves (see the examples above).

    You may not be able to identify these "moves" without the help of your partner. If you struggle to find these moves and the piece has an abstract, you may find them there as well. Note that the moves might occur several times and they may not occur in this order.

2. Do they make them in order? Are they short or long? Are they repeated? How much citation is included in establishing the territory?

3. Talk with your partner about what you found. Do they agree with your analysis of where the moves are made? Compare how each of your articles makes these moves and where. What do these choices tell you about the values and priorities of each of your fields?

Making and Supporting Persuasive Arguments

Most disciplinary genres are intended to argue or persuade—to convince a funding agency, to assert and illustrate a new analysis, to show how something that the writer has done or learned contributes to knowledge-making in the field. Writers must accomplish a number of things if their disciplinary texts are to be persuasive. For example, readers must be persuaded that an observation is a worthwhile contribution. To make such worthwhile observations, writers must know what issues are seen as relevant within fields and how to address them (what topics or problems are seen as current and relevant and which are not, for instance); how to contextualize results (what sources need to frame the ideas being discussed); what people in their community see as a convincing or "logical" argument, what theories or conceptual frameworks are currently accepted and how explicitly those frameworks must be described; what methodologies are considered sound; and what will be recognized as compelling evidence. All of these are quite field-specific and sometimes even sub-field-specific (Hyland, 2013).

Activity 3.4: Arguments and Evidence

Read your partner's article a bit more closely and ask:

1. What argument is the writer making? Where do they make it, and how explicit is it?
2. What evidence is used to support the argument? Is the course of the evidence textual? Observation? Personal? Qualitative? Quantitative? Several of these things? All of them?
3. Can you identify what kinds of theories and methodologies are employed? How explicitly are they described?

You may need some help from your partner to identify these elements.

After you each have some notes, compare your findings. How do arguments, evidence, theories, and methodologies work in similar or different ways across your two articles (and fields)?

This is a good time to reflect on the instructions you give your students when assigning them to write about research. Do you ask them to "back up claims with evidence," for example? If so, consider: how do you define what counts as evidence in your course? How is your view of evidence different from the way your partner defines what counts? You might realize that more refined definitions of evidence will be helpful for students in both courses. In addition to including what is perceived as relevant content, academic writers who want to be persuasive in communities of practice must also use social and linguistic conventions that others in their communities of practice find convincing. These include terms and phrasing that others in their community use, as well as the appropriate tone or register (a word linguists use to refer to the choice of written language that is used to communicate in a particular context) (Berkenkotter et al., 1988). Writers must also figure out how or if to represent themselves and their readers in the text. For example, do authors refer to themselves directly, not at all, or in third person? Are readers treated as present or ignored? Are they imagined as friendly or hostile? Disciplinary communities of practice vary greatly in this regard, and even different journals or book series within one field might vary. These rhetorical choices are all part of the way a writer demonstrates their credibility and persona (or ethos), what is seen as the appropriate balance of confidence and deference given their positionality, the level of claim they are making, and their evidence.

Once again, you might pause to reflect here on the implications for your students of what you are discovering. Are you expecting them to use phrases and terms or grammatical constructions (like passive voice) that may not only be unfamiliar to them but which they may be told not to use in some of their other courses? Do they need help navigating how to refer to themselves and to readers? If you say "cite other scholarship," do you need to help them understand how much is enough and how much is too much? Again, these expectations can differ quite a lot across fields.

Activity 3.5: Familiar and Unfamiliar Language

Return to the article your partner brought.

1. Circle examples of terms and phrases that you would not typically see in articles in your own field.

2. Focus on the article's author or authors. Are there one or many? How do the authors refer to or represent themselves—directly, indirectly, not at all? For example, does the author use "I," "we," "they," or use the passive voice to avoid naming a person as the agent of the work being discussed? Does the author discuss their positionality?

3. How does the author refer to or seem to imagine the readers? Are they addressed at all ("you" or "readers" or "other researchers")? If so, where and how? Does the writer seem to anticipate the readers will be charitable or hostile? How do you know? (For example, do they directly name possible counterarguments and try to refute them?)

4. Are there any clues as to how the author treats other scholars in relation to their own work? Is there an attitude of deference? Is there an effort to cite a great deal of other scholarship or very little? Are other scholars treated combatively? Are other scholars ignored altogether in favor of just discussing "facts"?

Take notes and then discuss what you found with your partner. This is a good time to ask your partner to serve as an "insider informant," perhaps explaining whether what you highlighted is typical for the field, for one journal in the field, or maybe just for this writer. Your partner might also explain why certain conventions are used (for example, the passive voice or not naming other scholars in the text itself).

Source Use and Citations

Instructors are often concerned that student writers don't know how to incorporate and cite sources. This concern feels commonsensical, reflecting the belief that it should be fairly straightforward to cite any sources students use beyond "common knowledge" within their papers, and then create a reference list at the end.

But as you may have already seen by looking at your partner's research article, using sources and citing them is far more complicated. Understanding why brings together several of the threshold concepts you have explored thus far in this book.

- First, writing is a social activity whose value is determined and reinforced by audiences, in this case audiences within your field (Roozen, 2015c).
- Second, writing mediates activities through recognizable and recurring forms—such as ways of incorporating and citing sources (Russell, 2015).

- Third, writing is a means of learning and creating new knowledge—but in this case, that knowledge must be carefully chosen and intentionally used (Estrem, 2015).
- Fourth, writing is informed by prior experiences. By the time college students reach your course, they have likely had a number of lessons (potentially contradictory ones) about sources and citations (Lunsford, 2015b ; Roozen, 2015c; Yancey, 2015).

The accumulated lessons of these threshold concepts, along with the idea that "source use and citations are aligned with disciplinary values," lead to important questions you should consider when asking students to write about research and/or simply write with sources. First among them: what sources are acceptable? For instance: is personal experience considered a source? Ethnographic data? Novels? Numbers? Is it acceptable to cite scholars from other fields or not?

Then there is the question of what counts as "common knowledge," since "common knowledge" is often identified as something that doesn't require citation (in some fields). But what is common to a long-time member of a particular research community is decidedly not common to an 18-year-old in an introductory course (Shi, 2011). Textbooks in such introductory classes tend to summarize ideas without citing their sources. Can students do the same? Are they expected to cite the textbook? Find the original sources? Or assume these ideas are simply "common knowledge"? "Citing sources" is a shorthand for an extensive practice associated with knowledge building within fields. The texts we create and the ones we ask students to produce are expected to build on or otherwise be connected to other texts—to have a meaning that is relative to those other texts, too (a practice that writing scholars call intertextuality [Dryer, 2015; Porter, 1986; Roozen, 2015a]).

Then there is the thorny problem of citation itself. In high school English classes, where students do a good bit of their writing, they typically learn Modern Language Association (MLA) citation format: author is named in the body of the writing (e.g., Jane Austin described longing....") , year is less important and often not important at all. Quotations are extended, often 1–2 paragraphs. References at the end of the paper are listed in alphabetical order, with the publication year at the end of the citation. But these rules (or conventions) reflect the beliefs and values of the people who create, use, and maintain the system: in this case, the Modern Language Association, the disciplinary association of literature and languages. These include the belief that literary works that are "timeless," that the author of the work is the most important feature; that it's necessary to include fairly extensive source material from a text to support interpretation of its meaning. These conventions are quite different from citation conventions in fields like history or biology, where timeliness is extremely important, or engineering, where ideas and findings are often more important than either date or scholar (D'Angelo et al., 2016; Karatsolis, 2016).

All of this use and citation of sources takes place within varied genres. Students need to know what and whom to read and cite (and how to cite), but also how to do this within the genres that mediate disciplinary or professional activity. Lab reports, field notes, literature reviews, book reviews, essays—each requires the writer to draw on sources differently as they enact the conventions of the genre and the field where it is mediating activity—and this gets even more complicated when we consider how citation works in formal texts outside the academy (Anson & Neely, 2010; Bazerman, 1987; Buranen & Stephenson, 2009; Connors, 1999; Hyland, 1999; Lerner, 2015).

To help students learn how to use and cite sources in the ways you expect, it's critical to untangle the complexities of attribution and recognize how closely related these practices are to the values of the field using them, as well as to understand disciplinary perspectives on those values. Disciplinary perspective is especially important to remember when you see unintentional violations of expectations of source use and citations. It is easy to view such violations as the student having betrayed ideas about intellectual property ("taking someone's ideas as their own") or disciplinary focus ("using sources that aren't right"). Many times, the perceived violations by students are more complex than simply a choice to cheat or plagiarize.

Activity 3.6: Knowing Who, What, and When to Cite

You'll complete this activity on your own, but share the results with your partner. Focusing on two courses you teach—one introductory and one advanced—reflect in writing on these questions about the courses:

1. What people or ideas are routinely cited in the disciplines or fields these courses relate to? Do students come into the courses already knowing about these people or ideas? How can you be sure?
2. What particular previous studies or texts do students in these courses need to be familiar with? How do they gain this familiarity? In other words, what do you think they should already understand as "common knowledge"?
3. How do students know what/who it is essential for them to cite when they write for these courses?
4. How do they know what ideas/sources/people are central to a particular conversation? That is, who must be cited, who shouldn't be cited?

After reflecting on these questions, talk with your partner. What are you recognizing about students' prior knowledge about important texts, ideas, and people? What are one or two supports you might build into your courses to help students gain the awareness they need?

Identifying expectations of what is typically cited (important people/ideas, previous studies/texts) and *how* those things are cited (how sources are incorporated, connections to meaning-making, how to indicate sources) are important steps in delineating practices associated with source use. These expectations and practices are often largely unfamiliar to undergraduates and beginning graduate students, who know less about values that orient and sometimes form the boundaries of disciplinary worlds.

In Activity 3.7, you will be asked to identify some of your assumptions about what gets cited and how. Not only do instructors have expectations about what is common knowledge and who should be cited, they also have expectations for what the attribution should look like in the text itself. For example, are other scholars named directly within texts, named only parenthetically, or not named at all? These practices are called "integral" and "non-integral" citation, with integral citations clearly naming authors within the sentence ("John Jones argues...") while non-integral citation either includes the name in parenthesis, footnote, or even only with a number that corresponds to a references list. While texts often use a combination of both, some fields adhere to one or the other more rigidly. Integral citations tend to be used in fields that value the contributions of individual thinkers; their names are mentioned in citations (so they are "integral" to the writing) and often include extended excerpts from texts. One study found that philosophy, for example, uses integral citation 64% of the time to accomplish its work, which "typically consists of long narratives and engages the arguments of other writers" (Hyland, 2004, p. 25). Non-integral citations are those that point to previous scholarship in a parenthetical or as part of a list of citations. Non-integral citations are often used in fields where accepted ideas or findings take more precedence, such as biology or engineering. Fields that primarily use non-integral citation may use a number system (referring readers to a list of citations in numerical order) at the end of the publication and rarely (if ever) include extended quotation from the source texts (Hyland, 1999, 2000, 2002; Maroko, 2013).

Fields also differ in how much of another text can be quoted directly (if at all) and how. Some fields (such as applied linguistics or sociology) allow for more extended direct quotations of other texts, while in other fields (like physics or engineering) writers rarely, if ever, do this (Hyland, 2004).

As you are likely discovering, directions such as "cite your sources" and "don't cite what is common knowledge" are often not specific enough for most students, especially in general education courses and courses taken early in a major. These sorts of expectations, while well-meaning, gloss the complexity of citation practices and their variations across fields. Until students learn what counts as common knowledge for your courses, which ideas you and your colleagues assume to be understood and which need to be attributed to specific people, and whether their written arguments in your class should focus on a person, an idea, or something else, they are likely to struggle.

Activity 3.7: Examining Citation Conventions

Return to the article your partner brought:

1. Mark instances of integral and non-integral citation.
2. Indicate which are used predominantly. Explain why.
3. Explain how work is usually cited—block quote, direct quote, summary, generalization?

Compare with your partner and discuss practices that most surprised you. Ask your partner to explain why these practices are used in their field

Activity 3.8: Making Expectations Explicit for Students

You've just spent time studying research writing in your field (and your partner's), as well as thinking about how you talk with students about elements of research based writing. Now, draw on what you have learned to start writing some explicit expectations and directions for your students.

1. Make a list of one-sentence findings from each of the reflective activities in this chapter (3.1–3.7).
2. Make notes to yourself about what you want to tell students (potentially at varying levels—new undergraduate, new graduate, advanced graduate) about research-based writing and citation based on what you've learned. You'll read more about talking with students later in this chapter, as well.

Stating Your Field's Writing Expectations for Students

In Chapter 2, you thought a good deal about some threshold concepts of writing and how they can help you start to study writing in your life and, especially, your disciplinary life. In this chapter, you looked especially closely at conventions of research-based writing, thinking about how conventions and genres for writing (particularly research writing) differ across academic fields. Now it's time to step back and think about the big picture. What is "writing" in your field? And what is "good writing"? And how can you talk about this with your students? Chapter 1 described the ways in which writing can serve as a gateway to disciplinary practice; it also emphasized the importance of providing *access* by making practices associated with disciplinarity (and writing) explicit and transparent. Stating your field's (or sub-field's) expectations is the starting point for providing this disciplinary access. That's because, as Chapter 1 noted, writing is never "just writing"—it's a representation of the values and ideologies that are important to you and to others with whom you feel yourself to be aligned (Lerner, 2015; Scott, 2015; Villanueva, 2015).

Once you've done this deep dive, it will be important to take a step back and put your reflections into practice, communicating with students about both *what* these practices are and *why* they are significant—maybe even *how* they have come to be, over time, and what they represent. This kind of explanation is referred to by some researchers as "pedagogical content talk" (Harrison et al., 2019; Seidel et al., 2015). This is classroom language you use to explain *what* the expectations are in clear and transparent terms, and also *how* expectations have come to be. It is even possible to explore whose voices have been more and less powerful in the process of creating these forms and conventions. Such awareness is important if you want to provide students access to your field because it shows them that conventions and expectations don't come from nowhere, but were created by particular people with particular identities, goals, and values.

As difficult as it is for instructors to navigate the rocky terrain of disciplinary persuasion, it is infinitely more difficult for our students at every level. Among other things, students need to:

- sort through, understand, and appropriately use specialized vocabulary,
- recognize and use specialized forms of argument,
- understand how people here establish credibility,
- know what prior work (who and what) to cite,
- know how to cite it appropriately,
- take the right stance as a writer, and
- address readers in appropriate ways.

Activity 3.9: Pedagogical Instructor Talk: Expectations for Writing in Your Field

Review what you wrote in the reflective activities for Chapters 2 and 3. Consider the conversations you had with your partner from a different field about similar and different expectations for writing in your two fields.

Drawing on these, write a short statement to your students (choose either undergraduate or graduate) that explains

1. what "writing" is in your field/profession/field;
2. what activities writing is mediating/facilitating there;
3. what people in that field view as the characteristics of "good" or "effective" writing and under what circumstances and why, and
4. what elements of writing in your field might surprise students who are new to it.

Be as specific as you can, and if the characteristics of good writing differ from one genre to another, explain that to be the case.

One way to show—and not just tell—students about the conventions of writing in your field is to provide them with some overviews of the expected conventions, accompanied by annotated examples of both student and professional papers. For example, Suzanne Kunkel, Kate de Medeiros, and Jennifer Kinney, gerontology faculty at Miami University, have developed the following explanation of what they expect from student writing:

What does Gerontology value in writing?

Being a gerontologist means more than just studying later life and applying methods to solve problems. It means having a "gerontological voice." That is, the field of social gerontology values applying knowledge and building theory using a social science lens.

- Writers are seen as credible when they present a conceptual context that draws from multiple disciplinary areas and demonstrate methodological sophistication and rigor. Papers should represent a "dialogue." The field's citations practices embody these values, and you can see that in the breadth of sources used, with specific citations from gerontology sources. Citations should be purposeful, strategic, and support the writer's argument/claim and avoid overgeneralizations, oversimplifications, and unfounded opinions.

Effective writing in social gerontology does the following:
- presents logical, parsimonious argument with neutral language
- uses standard signposts and structure
- avoids absolutes
- demonstrates respectful authority

Gerontology majors should expect to do the following:
- read thoroughly and critically
- finish synthesizing their reading before claiming their research space
- seek feedback appropriately
- be prepared to change their stance based on the feedback they receive
- participate in authorship discussions to understand the work of conceptualization, coherence, and contextualization as well as methods and results
- practice, practice, practice (improve, integrate, evolve)

They also then annotated an article from their field to show students what these "moves" look like in practice (see https://tinyurl.com/bdevyryv):

Figure 3.1. Effective writing in social gerontology.

You can view their guide on the Miami University website at https://tinyurl .com/bdevyryv.

This chapter has primarily focused on surfacing and naming your field's values, conventions, and practices around writing so that you can name them for students and invite them into your work. This is a necessary part of *inclusive* teaching. Sometimes inviting students to engage in the already-existing practices is not enough, however. If the conventions of a field exclude some ways of making and representing knowledge that would enrich and expand the field and its members, then instructors may want to consider how to also create *opportunities* for students to challenge and change some practices that either no longer serve or may not leave room for them to enter the field.

Conclusion

Most instructors have learned to embody their field's expectations in writing over quite extended periods of time and through a great deal of trial and error, receiving feedback from reviewers and advisors telling them they have left out important bodies of scholarship, used theories that are discredited, failed to employ a methodology correctly, or were too combative (or, conversely, not assertive enough). By the time instructors are able to successfully enact all of these textual moves in their own academic writing, those moves most likely feel like "common sense." One of the challenges for good teachers is to bring the conventions of writing in your field back from the realm of common sense and recognize how difficult and idiosyncratic those conventions can be for newcomers. The activities you engaged in across this chapter were intended to help you do this.

One caveat is in order here, however: you should not necessarily ask all of your students to write in the ways that people in your field write. In fact, there are classes where such expectations might be deeply inappropriate—for example in general education courses enrolling students who will never take another class in your field. Instructors sometimes expect all of their students to produce what they see as "good writing" (which is actually field-specific writing) because they mistake it for "academic writing in general"—and they may do this whether those students are intending to join their fields or not. If you can identify and name the features of texts that are specific to your field, you can also ask yourself whether some, all, or none of these conventions and rhetorical moves need to be made by which of your students—and in which courses—and for what reasons.

After completing these activities, you might identify some courses where you might want to adjust your expectations, focusing more on higher-level ways of thinking and practicing that might be useful to students across all fields and more popular genres, and focusing less on citation, format, and evidence that are specific to their own fields, which these students will never enter.

Naming what you already do does not mean you need to keep doing it, ask all of your students to do it, or embrace it without question. Instead, such naming helps you recognize what has previously been invisible to you, bring it to conscious awareness, contemplate it, and decide what you want to keep doing, do differently, or change altogether. Naming what you and your colleagues do through writing helps you gain the language for talking about what you see in student writing. This ability to name what you know and do is one step on the road to offering students *access*. As you name your field's written practices, you may also recognize features of writing—and thus, values, conventions, and power structures—that you dislike, find outdated or restrictive, or believe to be exclusionary. You might then have conversations with students about what the writing in your field values and prioritizes; who it invites in and who it excludes; and how they might work to change conventions that no longer serve. This facilitates *opportunity*, finding ways for students to bring their identities and commitments to ways of writing (and thinking) in your field. Chapter 4 focuses on how to learn more about your students and those ways of thinking, briefly shifting your field to *teaching writers*.

Preparing for Chapter 4

The next chapter will shift from a focus on *teaching with writing* to *teaching writers*. Take a minute before you dive in to record (in writing) what you are noticing and/or thinking thus far. You may want to refer back to these notes as you read and complete activities in the next chapter.

Chapter 4. Learning About and With Learners

While students have been mentioned consistently throughout the first three chapters of this book, you have so far largely focused your analysis on the contexts, purposes, and audiences for whom you've asked students to write. Chapter 1 asked you to identify ways of thinking in your field or discipline that are often tacit, then start connecting those foundational ways of thinking to expectations for writing. This emphasis on ways of thinking and connections to writing is the starting place for creating *access* to your field; that is, making the ways that the field "works" and how people participate in it more transparent. Chapter 1 explained that *access* is a key part of inclusive teaching. Chapters 2 and 3 helped you to delve into connections between epistemologies, ideas of "rightness" (and what's less "right") and genres and conventions of writing. Then, Chapters 2 and 3 asked you to complete activities that continue to create disciplinary access.

The chapters thus far have also emphasized that inclusive teaching involves creating *opportunity*—ways for students to bring their knowledge and commitments to your courses and even use those to push the boundaries of courses and fields in ways that represent different ideas and values. This happens as people make knowledge through writing; it also happens as people use writing to represent what they know. Creating *opportunity* for learners/writers, then, involves working from what students know: building on "funds of knowledge," the knowledge that learners bring from their everyday experiences (González et al., 2005; also see Yosso, 2005). These are *asset-based* approaches to teaching that focus on what students bring (e.g., Davis & Museus, 2019a, 2019b). Many other teacher-researcher-advocates—Paulo Friere (1970), bell hooks (1994), Gloria Ladson-Billings (2021), Mike Rose (1989), to name a few—have enumerated the importance of recognizing what people bring and *can* do (vs. *can't* do). This chapter provides a way to learn about learners and build on their strengths as part of an asset-based practice. We recognize that for some instructors this might seem familiar ("I do that all the time!"); for others—especially those teaching large, lecture-based courses—it might seem more challenging. That's why, in this chapter, you will gain practical strategies that use writing (both your own and your students') to learn about learners and build our asset-based approaches.

Empathetic Knowledge

The approach outlined here is rooted in taking action based on *empathetic knowledge*—knowledge that is formed *with*, not *about*, learners (Campelia, 2017). The activities in previous chapters should have illustrated this in your own experience; for example, that your ideas about what makes writing "good" come from your experiences as a person and a professional. The same is true, of course, for students, who bring considerable experience with writing and as writers to your courses. Their experiences are *different* from yours and might be *different* than what you expect—but they are as important to your students as your own experiences are to you. Enacting empathetic knowledge can help you reflect on your experiences again, learn more about what students bring to writing, and cultivate an asset-based practice that will provide access and opportunity for those students.

Goals for this chapter include:

- developing a practice of empathetic knowledge by
  ◦ studying your own learning experiences and assumptions
  ◦ creating concrete strategies to get to know about students' interests, commitments, and identities
- identifying elements of asset-based approaches to teaching (of writing)
- analyzing course materials/foci to find places to create opportunity (through writing and thinking), enabling them to bring their ideas (through writing) to our courses and possibly fields.

Forming, Confirming, and Identities: Why?

Earlier chapters have demonstrated that your experiences both contribute to and are informed by your disciplinary or professional identities. They also suggested that ideas about "good writing" reflect values and ideologies that are connected to those identities. As instructors across disciplines seek to make fields, professions, and institutions more inclusive, it is important to invite in those whose experiences have been marginalized or dismissed previously, such as students who are part of historically excluded groups, low-income students, first-generation students, LGBTQIA+ students, and others. Research shows that people in these populations regularly experience:

- *Stereotype threat*: Initially defined by Claude Steele, stereotype threat "refers to the tension that arises in members of a stereotyped group when they fear being judged according to stereotypes" (Ambrose et al., 174).
- *Implicit bias*: Unconscious but socially-reinforced generalizations that are often accompanied by assumptions about beliefs, perspective, ability, and other attributes.
- *Microaggressions*: Repeated actions (including words) that reflect discriminatory beliefs and undermine a person's agency

Each of these practices reflect and perpetuate systemic injustices—racism, sexism, homophobia, religious bias, classism, raciolinguicism (Rosa & Flores, 2017). These injustices deny students the ability to contribute to the discipline.

Creating *opportunity* in courses, making room for others' identities and commitments in order to form and confirm knowledge with them before, during, and after writing, can help to counteract these injustices. This means providing students with opportunities to create new knowledge that you (as a community of practice expert) might not be able to create—because what you see and know is also shaped by your own identities and biases. By creating opportunity, you ensure that there is room within disciplinary practices and knowledge for the identities students bring, broadening the bases for what is considered "good." As an example, consider what happens when an engineering student from an Indigeneous group contends that the narratives of people who live near a proposed dam are important pieces of data and evidence. Engineers typically do not consider narrative as data. Yet in this case, the Indigenous student brings a powerful perspective and demonstrates why narrative might sometimes be important data to consider when solving an engineering problem. Doing so expands the purview of what is included in the planning, and engineers may begin paying greater attention to the narratives of those affected by their work, something that has typically fallen outside of engineering practice (and has, instead, been seen as being the work of anthropology, public health, or sociology).

Taking class time to learn more about students might feel daunting, given everything else you need to accomplish. But as David Asai (2019), Senior Director for Science Education at the Howard Hughes Medical Institute notes, teaching is a human profession. If you don't take time to get to know the people in your classes, you miss out on new contributions from previously excluded learners. Additionally, peoples' feelings of belonging are closely linked to academic engagement, persistence, and achievement. (For a review of this literature, see Pekrun & Linnenbrink-Garcia, 2012). Students come to instructors with the rightful expectation that courses (and contacts) will help them to continue their intellectual, civic, professional, and personal development through a process of learning—so in many ways, instructors have a responsibility to respond to learners as people.

Enacting Empathetic Knowledge

As noted earlier, enacting empathetic knowledge entails "forming and confirming" knowledge with others. Adapting ideas from researchers who study and engage others in enacting empathetic knowledge provides faculty with a framework for action.

Synthesizing ideas from Georgina Campelia (2017) and Sara Ahmed (2018), it's possible to identify six steps to build empathetic knowledge:

- Element 1: Knowing Yourself: understanding your own expertise and experiences as a learner
- Element 2: Naming Contexts: situating experiences, expertise, and identities in communities of practice (e.g., disciplinary contexts)—your own and others'

- Element 3: Learning About Others' Perspectives
- Element 4: Reflecting on Your Perspectives
- Element 5: Creating Opportunities: "forming and confirming knowl-edge" (Campelia, 2017) with others
- Element 6: Building Structures: creating workable boundaries (for you and for students) to enact empathetic knowledge

The activities in this chapter will enable you to practice applying each of these elements to your own classrooms.

Element 1: Knowing Yourself

You have already spent some time in earlier activities identifying your experiences with *writing* in your disciplinary context. In Activity 4.1, you'll reflect on your experience *as a learner*. This kind of reflection serves as a reminder of particular moments of struggle you may have forgotten, and helps you identify who hindered and helped in those moments, how, and why.

Reflecting on a moment of difficulty around a hard idea can help you identify the idea and how you worked with it. It might also help you identify others involved and the roles they played. As an expert, you have worked through a number of learning challenges, and your identities and situatedness have played a role in how you were able to handle these challenges. The first step of the practice of empathetic knowledge is recognizing that as experts and teachers, most instructors have encountered moments of difficulty and both instructors and students benefit when everyone understands how they were able to maneuver within and around those challenges.

Activity 4.1: Knowing and Naming Your Learning Experience

1. Write about the first time you can remember encountering an idea, ideally in your field, that was really difficult for you.
2. Next, reflect on how (or if) you got a handle on the idea. Who helped you with it? Who hindered you? What did they do, and how did what they did contribute to or inhibit your work with the concept? How did your identity or identities come into play in this process of engagement with another? Once you feel like you started to move toward understanding of the idea—once you "got it" or even started to grasp pieces of it—what was that like?

Element 2: Naming Contexts

The second step in the practice of empathetic knowledge is to situate your own experiences and expertise within your field (community of practice). This builds on thinking you've done in previous chapters as you've closely analyzed the connections between your ideas about "good writing" and that field. Here, you will conduct a close analysis of some of the language you used to describe the experience. The words that experts use tend to be packed with meanings that make implicit sense to the expert insider, but which are not always explored or explained for novice learners. For example, you might have experienced a "Eureka!" moment when you worked through a challenge. By looking more closely at the language you to describe that feeling, you can identify what it meant for you to do something in ways that were expected and also name feelings associated with that way of operating.

Activity 4.2: The Words You Use to Explain What Is Expected

Using the reflection you wrote for 4.1, circle the most prominent or striking descriptors associated with:

- the emotions that you've described in initially encountering the idea
- working through the challenge
- the key actions and/or language you described in conjunction with your recollection about who/what helped or hindered
- the language you used to describe the experience of coming through the moment

It's likely, maybe even probable, that much of what you're going to circle will be verbs (feelings, actions, activities . . .). Whatever you come up with, keep a list of what you identify in your reflection on part 1 of the activity. Ideally, you've started to learn about your own learning, especially the affective portion of that learning—and some of the emotions associated with that learning. This can help to remind you what it was like *for you.*

Element 3: Learning About Others' Perspectives

Activities 4.1 and 4.2 should have helped you recall some of your own experience as learners, potentially even reminding you about aspects of learning that you hadn't remembered until you started writing about them. The next step in the practice of developing empathetic knowledge is to learn about students' perspectives and experiences, especially the knowledge, commitments, and other assets that they bring to your classes. One easy way to do this is by surveying students. Even in the largest classes, you can create a survey using questions adopted from literacy educator Gholdy Muhammad (2020).

Activity 4.3: Learning about Others' Perspectives

Pick a class that you are teaching this term and create an online survey (using something like SurveyMonkey or Google forms). Give the survey to your class and collect responses for the next set of activities. Ask students some or all of the following questions:

- What would you like me to know about you as a learner?
- How do you learn best?
- How is <this course/field> important to you?
- If you could tell me something to help me understand the connection between this course and what's important to you, what would it be?
- What's something you do really well or are very proud of?
- How could this course support your future goals?
- What's one question you have about this course?
- What's something you think might be challenging about this course? How have you approached similar challenges before?

Once you receive responses to the survey, you can use what you learn to engage with the next element of empathetic knowledge.

Element 4: Reflecting on Your Perspectives

Students' responses to a survey like this can provide some insight into learners' commitments and perspectives. As you read them, they might prompt agreement, questioning, or other conscious or unconscious responses—you might be surprised about something learners are proud of, or think that something that they find challenging about the course is something that they should know, for instance. If (or when) this happens, you might also find that you have sometimes unconsciously acted on your assumptions about what students know or have experienced. For instance, faculty often find that their students seem to know less about a subject than the instructors feel that *they* did at the same point in their college careers. They might then cover what they think students *should* know. But they also might make assumptions about students' abilities. This might lead them to leave out important review materials or suggest through comments that if students don't know something, they are behind or in need of remediation. While the faculty member may intend these comments to be helpful, showing students what is necessary for success in the field, students might receive them differently: as indications that the faculty member does not believe in their abilities, or that the faculty member does not believe in the abilities of students who are like them (a form of stereotype threat).

Activity 4.4 asks you to take a look at your own responses to see what you learn about students. Externalizing and observing can help you to meet students where they are (rather than where you think they are or should be). Then, bringing in ideas from previous chapters, you can design or redesign courses to help students develop the knowledge and experiences you think are important for success. It's also useful to note that especially when students participate in sequential courses, this might require looking well beyond just one course to an entire sequence within a department, or even across multiple departments.

Activity 4.4: Externalizing and Observing Your Responses

Reviewing students' surveys, start to put selected responses into a chart, as below:

Surprising or unexpected findings	Why the findings surprised you/were different from what you expected	Unsurprising or expected findings	Why you expected what you found

Element 5: Creating Opportunity

Analyzing your reactions to students' experiences and perspectives is another step toward creating opportunity, especially as you consider how those reactions compare to your own experiences as a learner. Creating opportunity also means making space for these different ways of approaching or thinking about a subject or a discipline. This can happen in many areas; there are many books and articles that discuss the importance of diversifying curriculum and using inclusive pedagogies. Since the focus of this book is *writing*, here you will be asked to reflect on how you create opportunity in some of the written artifacts that you provide students. Such written artifacts can create space and opportunity for students to bring their ideas, identities, and commitments to learning.

For Activity 4.5, focus on a document you've created for an undergraduate class (if possible), such as an assignment or a syllabus. You will use this artifact to identify where you include the kind of helpful pedagogical explanations discussed at the end of Chapter 3, and to study the perspective on learners in the document. For this, you will especially focus on where and whether the document reflects a deficit-based perspective and/or an asset-based perspective. Deficit thinking reflects a *"blame the victim* orientation" and often "emerge[s] in language that treats people as problems" (Davis & Museus, 2019b, np). For instance, some examples of deficit thinking include the idea that "grit" or individual determination is the key to success, or that students need "bootstrapping" or "bootcamp" learning to "close the achievement gap" between prior experience and what they "need to know" to succeed. In course documents, deficit-based perspectives can be reflected sometimes in language about atten-tion ("You must put your cell phones away in this course and pay attention. This is not a time for online shopping."), or intellectual property ("Instances of cheating will result in an immediate failure of the assignment and reporting to the student judicial office"). Deficit-based perspectives and language convey a belief that learners have a deficit (of knowledge, of responsibility, of commit-ment) and the institution's responsibility is to close it by helping students "try harder" or enact different "attitudes."

Asset-based thinking is the opposite of deficit thinking; it places responsi-bility for inequity on the educational system and its elements (from instructors to curriculum to testing to pedagogy), then focuses on how to build on what learners bring to their learning. This is illustrated when instructors welcome stu-dents into a class; clearly outline what will be learned and why; invite students to reflect on what they know about the subject already, and describe how the course can build on students' prior experiences and help them advance their commit-ments. Importantly, asset-based language doesn't mean that you provide noth-ing but relentless encouragement. All learners, and especially learners who have been excluded or experienced bias, benefit from messages that affirm challenge, acknowledge struggle, and express confidence—for instance, "These are high standards! But we will work together, as a class, when we encounter moments of struggle, and the TAs and I are here to support you every step of the way" (see Cohen et al., 1999, for instance).

Activity 4.5 can help you to identify where your language starts to invite stu-dents to bring their knowledge and commitments to class. It might also show you where your language unconsciously reflects a deficit-based framework or some of the judgments that you identified earlier. If this is the case, it might point to places where you want to make changes. Fortunately, there are resources available to help. For example:

- USC's syllabus checklist (https://tinyurl.com/2p8ax36u)
- University of Michigan's inclusive syllabus language (https://tinyurl.com/d4evkaf4)
- Ann Marie Womack's Accessible Syllabus project (https://www.accessiblesyllabus.com)

Books like *What Inclusive Instructors Do* (Addy et al., 2021) also focus on inclusive and equitable teaching strategies; texts like *From Equity Talk to Equity Walk* (McNair et al., 2020) focus on broader department- and campus-wide activities with a focus on creating space for students, as well.

Language in syllabi and assignments contributes in important ways to mak-ing space for opportunity. Researchers hypothesize that using welcoming lan-guage can help mitigate stereotype threat, lead to the perception by students that instructors are more accessible and contribute to students' feelings of belonging and confidence (e.g., Cohen et al., 1999; Hammond, 2014).

Activity 4.5: Language Review

Focusing on the course document you've selected, use the checklist below, adapted from studies of non-content talk referenced in Chapter 3 (Harrison et al., 2019; Seidel et al., 2015) to identify the presence (or absence) of particular kinds of language:

Present?	Category	Asset-Based Perspective Example
	Demonstrating respect for students	"People bring different experiences and knowledge to this question: I want to value what you bring in."
	Revealing (course related) secrets	"You don't need to copy the slides in lecture—those are posted. Instead, write down things you want to remember, things you want to ask, things that seem important."
	Boosting self-efficacy	"Your ideas are important for this assignment/activity because _____."
	Preframing/ Connecting to key concepts	"This assignment/activity is a way for you to practice with <this/these key concepts>."
	Practicing <disciplinary> habits of mind	"This assignment/activity will reinforce the ways that you think like a <disciplinary participant>."
	Reinforcing community	"As you work on <activity/assignment>, be sure to talk/work with others."
	Using student work to drive choices	"It's due Sunday night no later than 6 p.m. so I can read it before I finish planning, because I want to be sure to be responsive to your thinking."
	Connecting <field> to "real world" and career/Fostering learning for the long term	"Completing <this> will also reinforce connections you're making between <this> and life outside of/beyond school, too. That's because _____."

While the categories included in this rubric in Activity 4.5 aren't the only ones that make space for opportunity, they provide a starting place for you to identify where and how your written documents reflect an asset-based, welcoming approach to teaching. From this initial examination, you can then consider other language, whether written or spoken. Figure 4.1, created by Sarita Shukla et al. (2022, p. 2), also provides a very useful summary of how deficit- and asset-based approaches lead to different framing of outcomes, which may contribute to your thinking beyond writing, as well:

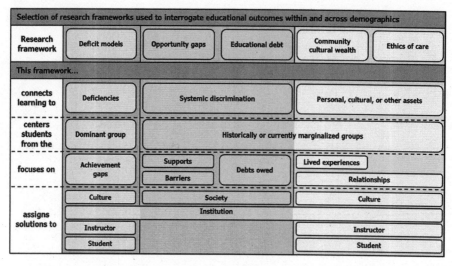

Selection of research frameworks used to interrogate educational outcomes within and across demographics				
Research framework	Deficit models	Opportunity gaps	Educational debt	Community cultural wealth	Ethics of care
This framework...					
connects learning to	Deficiencies	Systemic discrimination		Personal, cultural, or other assets	
centers students from the	Dominant group	Historically or currently marginalized groups			
focuses on	Achievement gaps	Supports / Barriers	Debts owed	Lived experiences / Relationships	
assigns solutions to	Culture	Society		Culture	
	Institution				
	Instructor			Instructor	
	Student			Student	

Figure 4.1. How deficit- and asset-based approaches lead to different framing of outcomes. (Shukla et al. 2022. Used with permission.)

Looking at language, especially as you consider how that language reflects orientations toward students, is one way to create opportunity for students in your courses. A second approach is ensuring that your curriculum—course readings, textbooks, and materials you provide for students—represent diverse creators and perspectives. D. L. Stewart refers to this practice as "creating space: ensuring that curriculum includes diverse authors, as well as creating classroom space for people to share their ideas" (UERU, 2020). Writing activities can be designed to invite learners to bring their ideas (and even their identities) in the context of your discipline or field. These writing activities can be understood along a continuum. On one end are activities that are closely focused on what is sometimes referred to as *writing to learn (WTL)*. These provide students a chance to *practice with important knowledge*: key or threshold concepts, theories, methods, or approaches to problem-solving, for instance. On the other end of the spectrum are activities focused on what is called *learning to write (LTW)*. LTW activities focus on *using important features of written genres in the field*—for instance, producing a hypothesis or generating research results or incorporating evidence using the specific genre conventions expected in the course or field. (Chapter 5 will look more closely at various uses of writing.)

Creating WTL and LTW writing activities, which provide ways for students to practice with existing ideas and ways of writing, can also enable students to bring their knowledge and identities to a course. For instance, in large (120+ student) courses, instructors have incorporated structured writing/peer review activities that invite students to practice defining key concepts and discuss why and how they are relevant in students' every day experience. You'll find examples of peer review assignments like this from chemistry and international relations in the Chapter 4 appendix.[4] Other efforts like Stem Cells Across the Curriculum (https://stemcellcurriculum.org) provide students with case studies such as HeLa cells and HPV genes and Stem Cells and Policy, then ask them to use writing (and other communication modalities, such as speaking and role playing) to define key scientific (as well as ethical) concepts, make connections between evidence from a variety of sources, traditions, and fields, and wrestle with the implications of the various perspectives on the history and use of stem cells (also see Chamany & Tanner, 2008).

This idea of defining and connecting key concept to students' commitments reflects Stewart's conception of "diverse and inclusive" teaching: it creates pathways for students to bring their identities to existing content knowledge, to think through connections between that content knowledge and things that they care about, and to situate what they believe is important in their day-to-day experience. This is an important step in creating disciplinary opportunity—that is, ensuring that diverse perspectives, ideas, and even ideologies contribute to disciplinary practice. Communication professor Walid Afifi modeled this when he described what happened after he asked students about the structure of a course they were taking in the middle of the term because he wanted to model the threshold concept of "reciprocity:"

> I sort of landed on this concept of reciprocity with communities . . . the idea . . . that we work on everything communally and I'm not bringing my expertise to them. . . . And literally as we were talking about this idea about our communities we're working with I said what would it look like if I fully applied that ethic to this class? And I had them write [about what we were doing and what they wanted to do] and turn in stuff. My TA read [what they handed in] and said [students seemed to be complaining]. But I tried to pause and say . . . let's really honor them, which is what I was trying to do . . . [As a result of taking their feedback seriously], I changed the syllabus organization. I changed the number of assignments. I changed the type of assignments. I changed about a third of the things that I did . . . I really sort of pushed the idea of honoring students as a community myself, and how well I was doing that or not as part of this class. . . . (as quoted in Adler-Kassner, 2019, p. 52).

As Professor Afifi demonstrates, creating opportunity can also involve pushing the *boundaries* of disciplinary values and ideologies so that they reflect a variety of ideas, identities, and ideologies. William Spriggs, professor of economics

---

4. In addition to linking directly to resources on the web, we provide archived versions of the materials in the appendix on this book's web page at https://wac.colostate.edu /books/practice/expertise.

and member of the Minneapolis Federal Reserve Board of Governors, pushed this boundary even further, addressing the construction of his field (economics) in an open letter to economists urging the field to study the "deep and painful roots" of modern economics, which includes "a definition of race that fully incorporated the assumed superiority of [white, Anglo-Saxon Protestants] and bought into a notion of race as an exogenous variable" (Spriggs, 2020, p. 1). Spriggs goes on to suggest that this foundational assumption means "racial differences cannot be objectively approached. The model begins with a fallacy that assumes racial differences as a natural order. It biases the model, because there is a built-in excuse for disparities that cannot be solved" (Spriggs, 2020, pp. 1–2).

Disciplinary associations like the Ecological Society of American, the Society for American Biological Educational Research, the American Historical Association, and others have over the last several years examined their disciplinary roots and provided curriculum and pedagogy focused on inclusive and equitable teaching.

In literacy education, which includes our field of composition/writing studies as well as English education, many teacher-researchers have renewed calls for faculty to reject the teaching of White Mainstream English (WME) as a normative discourse. Rather than teach students—especially students whose home dialects are not WME, such as those who use African American English (Baker-Bell, 2020, uses the term Black Language [BL])—to code-switch between dialects, teacher-scholars advocate for composition and English language arts teachers to create classes where students can study "anti-Black linguistic racism and white linguistic supremacy" (Baker-Bell, 2020, p. 2). This includes studying the grammatical features and rhetorical uses of Black Language; examining instances of raciolinguicism (i.e., personal judgments based on language and race; discriminatory practices based on language and race) (Charity Hudley et al., 2021); and engaging students in assignments that "move . . . students toward thinking about developing agency, taking a critical stance, and making political choices that support them in employing Black language for the purposes of various sorts of freedom, including dismantling Anti-Black Linguistic Racism" (Baker-Bell, 2020, p. 86). This approach to teaching writing (at the K–12 and/or college level), then, explicitly invites students to study and push against norms of WME, including WME as it is modified and employed in disciplinary genres. Instead, it invites students to bring their identities and commitments to writing, creating new ways of defining standards for what makes writing "good" or "right."

How instructors elect to create opportunity in your courses to form and confirm knowledge with students will depend on many things—beliefs about the purposes of writing (in your fields and professions and beyond them, as well); stances toward language and language use, and more. The strategies in this chapter will help to identify your own beliefs, values, and perspectives, learn more about those of students, and deliberately consider how to learn *about* and *with* learners in systematic ways.

Conclusion

This chapter has built on previous chapters in order to help you consider not only what your field already knows, does, and values (through its threshold concepts, values, and conventions of language use), but also to consider what it *could* know, do, and value by inviting in the perspectives and experiences of diverse learners. It has invited you to think about what students bring with them, and how their identities, feelings, and prior knowledge influence their ability to participate and learn in your classrooms. By examining your own attitudes and language in course materials, and remembering your own experiences as a learner, you can better ensure that all learners find a supportive environment where they can thrive—and also contribute new knowledge to your field.

Preparing for Chapter 5

The next chapter invites you to apply all that you have learned throughout this book and consider specific aspects of learning theory and writing research in order to redesign aspects of one course. Before you begin reading, review the notes you made for yourself at the end of Chapter 3. Supplement these with any connections you've made to learning about the writers in your classes after concluding this chapter.

Chapter 5. Structuring Intentional Learning Across Your Courses

By now, you've probably started to see how writing is a social activity that can contribute to learners' development in many ways. It can help students explore and situate themselves within the community of practice of your field when you *teach with writing*; it can help writers develop their thinking and show what they know when you *teach writing*. As Chapter 4 emphasized, writing also can be a way for you to connect with your students as people and as learners—*teaching writers*—because writing is tied to identity and experience. All of this occurs when you understand the roles that writing can play for students in enabling them to join the community of practice that is constituted by your field and in which you participate and create ways for students to connect with and even push those boundaries, providing both *access* and *opportunity*.

While previous chapters have included moments of application, this chapter asks you to put all your ideas into practice, structuring effective learning environments by relying on what scholarship tells us about how learning works.

Goals for this chapter include:

- clarify the nature of learning, especially how learning works for novices
- situate your course and writing within a learning framework
- learn how to scaffold for learning
- provide opportunities for you to rethink specific elements of your courses and assignments, including assignment design and feedback

To accomplish these goals, focus on one course as you work through the activities in this chapter. This way, you can dig deeply into assignments, activities, and the learning environment you want to design for that course. It might be most effective if you choose a course that has proven difficult for students or frustrating for you. You're going to use this course to dig into students' prior learning experience, outline course goals, and consider how you'll design the course keeping both of those in mind. It's important to emphasize at the outset: The steps you'll take in this chapter will primarily facilitate *access*, making knowledge-creating practices (especially writing) in your field more visible, and creating scaffolded strategies to support students' work with those. As this book has emphasized, providing access is essential; learners need to know how knowledge-creating works and how fields operate in order to write successfully in courses. But as the previous chapter demonstrated, without *opportunity*, access is simply another word for assimilation. Thus, the ideas in this chapter for creating access are necessary but not sufficient if your goal is to invite many kinds of learners into the work of your fields, and to be open to ways they may change the work of your fields.

Activity 5.1: A Challenging Course

Identify and collect your teaching materials for a course you teach where students frequently struggle or where you are often frustrated with student outcomes. A course where more students than usual receive grades of D, F, W, or Incomplete (aka "a course with high DFWI rates") would also be a good option. You will use this course throughout this chapter. For now, reflect briefly on why you think the course is challenging for students.

What is Learning?

Writing is always bound up with learning. The principle behind "writing to learn" (WTL) approaches (discussed in Chapter 4) is that writing can help people learn; the idea underscoring "learning to write" (LTW) is that learning is almost always demonstrated in some kind of composed knowledge (writing, mathematical figures, sound compositions, films). Because of the close connections between writing and learning, it's critical to reiterate some of the key ideas introduced throughout Chapters 1–4:

- Learning is a process that leads to change, which occurs as a result of experience and increases the potential for improved performance and future learning.
- Learning involves acquiring skills, practicing integrating them, and knowing when to apply what they have learned (Ambrose et al., 2010).
- Learning does not occur in a vacuum.

Deep learning, then, is *situated*—that is, it occurs in specific places. Deep knowledge about something occurs *in* a place. It requires not just knowing *what* (i.e., the "facts" or "formulas") but also knowing *how and why*—how and when to apply knowledge within the disciplinary or professional context. Thus, deep learning requires both declarative knowledge (knowing about) as well as procedural knowledge (knowing how)—and understanding how and why this knowledge matters and where else it can be applied. Declarative knowledge is "knowledge of facts and concepts that can be stated or declared," while procedural knowledge "involves knowing how and knowing when to apply various procedures, methods, theories, styles, or approaches" (Ambrose et al., 2010, p. 18). Procedural knowledge generally doesn't occur without declarative knowledge, but declarative knowledge *often* is separated from procedural knowledge, especially in school.

For instance, researchers studying introductory STEM courses have noted that those courses sometimes ask students to memorize things (periodic table, what meiosis is, principles of gravitational force), but don't as often ask students to apply those things in introductory courses (Mazur, 2009). Similarly, students in history classes are provided with dates and names associated with historical events, but are less often asked to situate these within broader contexts (Wineburg, 2018).

Activity 5.2: Goals for Your Course

Thinking of the course you identified in 5.1:

1. List the declarative knowledge you would like students to gain. What would you like them to know about by the end of the course?
2. Next, list what you would like students to be able to do with that knowledge by the end of that course (their procedural knowledge).
3. Finally, write a few sentences explaining why students need declarative and procedural knowledge and where and how both can be applied.

Experts, Novices, and the Challenges of Community of Practice

As this book has repeatedly emphasized, instructors are expert members of disciplinary and professional communities of practice. One feature of that expertise, in fact, is the ability to bring together declarative and procedural knowledge. In workplaces and other non-school communities (such as apprenticeships, clubs, etc), newcomers learn to move toward this kind of expertise by engaging in what Jean Lave and Etienne Wenger (1991) call legitimate peripheral participation— they begin by doing small things that are central to the work of the community and then move toward expertise and full participation. Paradoxically, schooling presents a challenge because it is not typically set up like a community of practice. In non-school communities of practice there are more oldtimers (experts) than newcomers (novices), and people are often focused on doing the work of the community (making shoes, selling insurance) rather than the learning goals of individuals. In school settings, there is typically one expert (the teacher) and many novices (the students) and the activity is "schooling" or individual learning. Thus, for classrooms to result in truly effective learning, the expert teacher needs to be aware of what novice students need to learn and then design careful learning experiences and opportunities to support that learning. As experienced teachers know, this isn't as easy as simply telling students, "Learn this, and then go and apply it." This is why learning researchers identify a difference between content expertise (being an expert in a subject) and *pedagogical* content expertise (Shulman, 1986).

Researchers note that teaching novices can be difficult because experts are typically not consciously aware of how they (as experts) do what they do—their practices have become *tacit*, and their perspectives *embodied*. They forget what it was like to learn declarative knowledge, combine or skip steps that turn that knowledge into practice, see patterns between elements of declarative knowledge that novices cannot see, and underestimate the amount of time tasks take novices to complete (Bransford et al., 2000). Experts are often operating at a level of unconscious competence (National Research Council, 2000; Shulman, 1986), not consciously or explicitly recognizing what they are doing or know how to do.

Take, for instance, the example of driving a stick shift. Experts know the "shape" of the gears (on the floor, on the steering column), know how to push the clutch and move the gearshift at the same time, and when to do so. They also have some sense of why it's necessary to do so, and how use different gears to do different things (e.g., shift up to reduce the number of rotations of the engine as the rate of speed increases, downshift to use the engine's force to slow the vehicle, use a lower gear when more torque is required, and so on). Once someone has mastered driving a stick shift, they do so without conscious effort or awareness and they can use their knowledge for more "advanced" purposes, like downshifting. Teaching someone else to drive a stick shift requires re-seeing all the steps involved and how one undertakes them, and then figuring out how to explain what to do—and providing safe opportunities for the learner to practice doing it herself.

Recognizing that experts know, do, and see things that novices do not can be an important revelation for teachers and students alike. One classroom activity that easily illustrates this point is asking everyone in the class, including the instructor, to write instructions for an activity that they are very good at. (The activity needs to require no special equipment.) Then, the class breaks off into pairs and each person completes the experience exactly as described in the instructions, but without asking any questions, one at a time. After the experience the activity completer describes what they wish they had known; the activity writer describes what they knew but forgot to include in the instructions.

Activity 5.3 asks you to reflect on your experience with a class in the same way the illustration above does with paired participants. You'll refer back to what you write in Activity 5.4, too.

Activity 5.3: Considering Students' Challenges

Continuing to focus on the course you chose for this chapter: think about times when you were surprised by how long it took for students (the majority of the class) to accomplish something, or when you realized that there were skills needed for the task you assigned that the majority of the students did not have. This might be related to (or the same as) the learning bottleneck that you identified in Activity 1.4 (in Chapter 1).

The Need for Scaffolding and How to Scaffold

When attempting to learn and apply new and difficult knowledge, learners benefit from working through an iterative process. In the literature (and practice) on learning, this is referred to as "scaffolding." Scaffolding so that students can build knowledge and skills does not mean you are avoiding rigor; it means providing access and inviting students into the rigorous, challenging work of your field by providing them with support. Scaffolding also requires providing students with feedback to help them improve their practice as they undertake that work (Cohen et al., 1999). One of the main goals of a rigorous learning environment, in fact, is to help students engage where tasks are too difficult for them to accomplish alone, but attainable with support and help (Vygotsky, 1978). If they can do the work by themselves with ease, they do not need a class to learn it. And if the material is too difficult even with help, then it is not pitched at the right level.

One goal of a rigorous but supportive learning environment is to design learning experiences that are scaffolded so that students can accomplish difficult tasks over time. This requires you as a faculty member to start with with the desired *end* result—the most conceptually sophisticated thing that students will need to show and/or know how to do—then designing learning that helps them learn and practice with the knowledge and skills they will need to use to achieve that result. (This is often referred to as "backward design" [Wiggins & McTighe, 1998]). Backward designing also requires you to recognize where your own expertise blinds you to what students don't know or can't yet do, so that you can build in learning opportunities to make the hard task possible.

Activity 5.4: What You Know/What's "Missing"

Referring to your reflection in Activity 5.3, identify what *you* know about this activity. How do you do it? What do you do before, during, and after the activity? Then, reflect on what is "missing" or you are not seeing in students' work with the activity. Since you've identified it as something that is difficult or took longer for a number of students, think about what they are not collectively "getting."

Activity 5.4 draws on elements of what "decoding the disciplines" research (described in Chapter 1) calls an "expertise interview." You may find it productive to undertake the activity with someone who can ask you to describe the moment(s) you're thinking about in some depth. But whether you complete it individually or on your own, it's safe to say that when you identify things that are "missing," you're beginning to also identify what you can build into your teaching to address students' challenges.

Identifying Course Goals, Outcomes, and Needed Skills

Once you've started to address elements that can address challenges, you can reflect on your course goals, outcomes, and the skills you want students to attain in the course. One way to do this is to identify a major, high-stakes course assignment and engage in some backward design in order to develop course activities, materials, and checkpoints that ensure students can complete the assignment. This entails identifying some major course outcomes and the related declarative and procedural knowledge students will need to achieve them, considering what assignments students might complete in order to gain this knowledge and meet course outcomes, and identifying the skills students will need in order to produce what you want them to.

For example, if one of your goals is for students to know about a general area of research in your field (course outcome, declarative knowledge) and to be able to explain major research trends in writing to others in the field (procedural knowledge), you might assign them to write a literature review (major assignment). What skills and knowledge do students need in order to accomplish writing an effective literature review for others in your field about a major research area? They need to be able to:

- find appropriate sources (use databases, know which ones are relevant to your field, understand how to use search times, understand what sources are credible and relevant);
- read sources (know how to read in ways you expect, take useful notes that lead to synthesis, and find important points in the sources);
- understand and summarize sources (know how to summarize, paraphrase, integrate source material into notes and summaries);
- synthesize sources (be able to compare ideas across sources, see patterns, make connections, and organize written materials); and
- write about ideas from across a variety of sources in ways that are appropriate for your field/field (identify themes and findings you see as relevant, find gaps in the literature, use terms and conventions your field uses, use citation as your field does).

As this example illustrates, to help students complete a difficult and meaningful task by the end of your course, you first need to uncover the invisible tasks and skills required to get there.

Activity 5.5: Identifying Major Course Outcomes and Related Skills

1. What is a major assignment that you give in the course you are focusing on in this chapter?
2. What are the learning outcomes students will achieve by completing this assignment?
3. Make a list of every skill or type of knowledge you can think of that students will need in order to successfully complete this major assignment.

Defining Your Terms

For students to achieve the outcomes you have defined and develop the skills related to those outcomes, it's also useful to ensure that you have defined key terms in the assignments and instructions. For instance, the previous section referred to a "literature review." This is a very specific genre, and you probably have a clear idea of what *you* mean when you ask students to produce it. Have you, though, defined the parameters of that genre for students? Often, faculty have very specific ideas as experts in a community of practice about what they mean when they refer to the genres that they'd like students to create. For instance, the term "theory" means different things in different disciplines; so do the words "model," "mechanism," and "change." And just as often, faculty do not share with students *their* definitions of the genres they ask students to write (what an art historian means by "essay," "research paper," or "literature review," for example). Laura Gonzales and colleagues documented this phenomenon in a short video (https://youtu.be/2SzMWLoR4C8), one that instructors often find very compelling (and troublesome) because it illustrates to them that because they are experts and have models in their heads of precisely what these things should be, they assume that their meanings are both shared and understood by everyone else (Mathew, 2014). This applies equally to terms that faculty use to refer to what should happen *in* these genres—activities like "analyze," or "describe," or "compare." These activities, too, have very specific meanings—but students, especially in introductory courses, rarely have insight into what the terms mean.

When faculty are asked to review key terms in one another's assignments, they invariably ask questions such as: "What does 'success' mean? What are the conventions of writing a sociology paper—what should it look like? Are there central principles that students will use to respond to the 'why' questions in this assignment? What should I know about case studies that are mentioned in the assignment?" When faculty members read the assignments written by other faculty members and even have a good deal of familiarity with those faculty members' courses, instructors from different disciplines tend to find they need more information about what is expected. Sometimes these explanations are a matter of a few sentences—but they are sentences that make a difference.

Activity 5.6: Defining Terms in an Assignment

In the same assignment you've selected for Activity 5.5, circle the key terms associated with what students need to do to complete the assignment. For example, these could be "write a research paper," or "analyze [these things]." Then, see where (or if) you have defined these things. If no definition is included, try to write one to two sentences for each so that students can understand the expectations of the assignment. Remember that you also should provide students opportunity to practice with these key terms/activities, especially if the assignment is "high stakes" or counts for a large portion of their grade.

Creating a Scaffolded Series of Low-Stakes Activities

Once you have defined the key terms and identified often-invisible skills and abilities students will need to complete your major assignment (and have taken inventory of the prior knowledge and experience they bring with them), you will want to create a scaffolded series of activities and assignments to help them accomplish the major task. In doing this, you will need to think explicitly about *high-stakes* and *low-stakes* assignments. A low-stakes assignment is worth few or no points or is counted as participation points; it may or may not be seen by the instructor and is primarily intended to support students as they work toward more high-stakes projects. A high-stakes assignment is worth considerable points in the course. It may consist of revisions of drafts that are more low stakes (worth fewer points), for instance.

To continue with the previous example of the literature review, Table 5.1 provides a list of skills students will need to write that genre, as well as a series of activities to help students gain (or review) those skills.

Table 5.1. Necessary Skills (An Example of Scaffolded Activities for a High-Stakes Assignment)

Skills/Knowledge Needed to Complete a Literature Review	Scaffolded Assignments & Activities
Finding sources (use databases, know which ones to use, how to search, qualifying sources)	Library activity: to learn how databases work, mini-activities to find sources on a topic that the full class shares (participation grade). Students complete heuristic to qualify the sources and compare with peers. Share a preliminary list of sources for their own project. (5 points)
Reading sources (how to read, take notes, find important points)	Read and annotate an article as a full class. (participation grade) Read and annotate individually; share with small group and compare understanding of a text. (5 points)
Understanding and summarizing sources	Students all summarize the same article, compare summaries, re-write summary based on comparison. (5 points) Complete annotated bibliography of some sources for their individual projects. (10 points)
Synthesizing sources	In small groups, students synthesize three articles they all read. Compare syntheses across groups. (5 points) Individually, create a chart of all their sources identifying areas of agreement, disagreement, and gaps in the research. (10 points)
Writing about these in ways appropriate for your field, ability to identify themes, findings, and gaps in existing research	Analyze three examples of good literature reviews. Write a list of characteristics of effective literature reviews, what they do and don't do. (5 points) Major high stakes assignment: complete literature review (50 points)

Note that in this example list of activities, students are working both alone and with others. They are often doing something as a group or full class before they try it individually. They are also, in every case, *actively* doing something rather than simply being told about it by the teacher. Learning is active. Telling is not teaching, and hearing is not learning. Students must attempt something and reflect on what they know with others. They need feedback along the way (though not always from the teacher) because learning is social. We will come back to the matter of feedback later in this chapter.

Try your hand at creating a series of low-stakes activities to scaffold the major assignment and outcomes you've identified.

Activity 5.7: Designing Activities to Support Major Learning Goals

Create a two-column table. Place the list of skills you identified in Activity 5.6 in the left-hand column. Then, in the right-hand column, brainstorm low-stakes activities or assignments that can help students either gain these skills or refresh their memories on what they already know.

Often in a learning environment, students view small activities and homework as "busy work." Thus, is it important to ensure that low-stakes assignments clearly build toward more difficult and high-stakes learning goals, and that students understand how the work builds. As activities and assignments are introduced, it can be helpful to explain how they connect to what students previously learned and did, and how they will build to what's next. Our course design strategies should be transparent to learners.

The Role of Prior Knowledge in New Learning

The preceding set of activities, as well as the activities in Chapter 4, likely reminded you that students do not come to our courses as blank slates. They come with extensive prior knowledge and experience about both course material and the kinds of writing we expect them to produce in the course. As Chapter 2 discussed, students also come with *different* prior knowledge, which can sometimes make designing the low-stakes activities (as you did in Activity 5.6) a challenge. Understanding what prior knowledge students bring with them is an essential part of designing a well-scaffolded learning experience. You can learn more about what students bring by asking them directly about their experiences and prior knowledge (for example, you can survey them, as Chapter 4 suggested).

At times, students' prior knowledge doesn't match the knowledge that instructors expect them to have. Activity 5.8 asks you to look back at previous iterations of your course (if there have been any) to consider what students know about a course.

Activity 5.8: Exploring Students' Knowledge and Beliefs

Focusing on the course you have been working with throughout this chapter, consider:

1. What do students typically know about the declarative content of the course when they enroll? What don't they know? What misconceptions do they often bring?
2. What experience do students typically have applying the kinds of content they will study in this course? What tends to be easy/hard for them, and why?
3. What do students typically think is the use value of the ideas and methods of this course when they enroll?

Your work in Activity 5.8 can build on what you learned by asking students what they bring to the course (from Activity 4.3). Sometimes, for instance, students' prior knowledge comes from a slightly different context—for instance, they might be enrolled in a biology course, but their experience with writing comes from a literature course. Students may have learned to write very well in a literature course and not recognize that the style and organization are inappropriate for a science course. Students also bring cultural assumptions and beliefs with them that may impede their ability to undertake the work of a particular course.

Addressing prior knowledge, especially when it doesn't match what is accepted in your field, might seem uncomplicated. But keep in mind that learning and writing are embodied—everyone believes what they believe (about a subject, about writing, or anything else) because they belong to communities of practice that reinforce and perpetuate those beliefs. When people enter into new communities and encounter different beliefs, those encounters can lead to what researchers refer to as "troublesome knowledge." As Chapter 4 demonstrated, dismissing students' prior knowledge has the potential to cause harm. But research has shown that you can mitigate these potential effects when you are very clear about what your field is, why the activities in your course are related to disciplinary knowledge and clear course goals, and why the knowledge that you want students to practice with and develop can contribute to their abilities to join (*access*) and change (*opportunity*) the field from the inside.

Even as you ensure that students' thinking is situated in *your* field's context by using clear language about what that context is and how the course activities reflect that context, sometimes prior knowledge can be hard to shift, as when inaccurate prior knowledge is conceptual. For example, students often believe that some people are just born good writers and others are not and that, because writing is hard for them, they are a bad writer for whom nothing can be done. This conception is difficult to change without activities, research, and reflective practice across time.

Students need to activate their prior knowledge for most effective learning. They need to recognize what they already know that is relevant and helpful in the current context, as well as what prior knowledge is not helpful or needs to be adapted. Quite often, students do not recognize that they already know things that can be brought to bear in the current context. Other times, students do not recognize that what they already know may not be appropriate or perhaps needs to be adapted.

Teachers can help students surface, name, and reflect on their prior knowledge and consider its relationship to the work of the current course. It's also possible to ask students about how they feel about this knowledge, especially bolstering the importance of that knowledge as they orient themselves to new learning. Quick writing prompts can, for instance, ask students to activate prior knowledge by:

- using writing as a "values affirmation" by asking students to reflect prior learning experiences in similar contexts, including describing what is challenging and how they overcame challenges (Binning et al., 2020; Miyake et al., 2010);
- providing "minor prompts and simple connections" to prior knowledge (Ambrose et al., 2010, p. 16; Bransford & Johnson, 1972; Gick & Holyoak, 1980);
- asking questions to "trigger recall" (Ambrose et al., 2010, p. 16; Woloshyn et al., 1994);
- asking students to draw on their own prior knowledge or experience to generate examples related to the new content they are learning (Ambrose et al., 2010; Peeck, et al., 1982); and
- asking students to actively create connections themselves rather than simply telling them what the connections are (Ambrose et al., 2010, p. 31).

Instructors can also talk to others who have taught the course or its prerequisites, give students a pre-course or pre-major unit survey like the one described in Chapter 4 to determine their prior knowledge and assumptions, ask students to complete an ungraded written reflection about their prior knowledge and experiences, or ask them to draw a concept map related to particular ideas (see Ambrose et al., 2010 for more ideas and details).

Often students' prior knowledge needs to be adapted, expanded, or repurposed in order to be usefully brought to bear on new knowledge and contexts. Research demonstrates that students are best able to adapt prior knowledge when they can say how that prior knowledge is "like" and "not like" what they are encountering now (Kim & Olson, 2020; Reiff & Bawarshi, 2011). For example, if they learned to write a five-paragraph essay in high school, they can be prompted to explain how some of the features of that text apply to their current history research paper (there need to be main claims supported by evidence) and how others do not apply (there are likely many more than three pieces of evidence needed and many more than five paragraphs (e.g., Perkins & Salomon, 2012; see also Yancey et al., 2014).

Activity 5.9: Activating Students' Prior Knowledge

1. Identify a major assignment or course unit where students typically struggle to draw on prior knowledge—either at all or appropriately. What problems do students generally have here?
2. Brainstorm two to three small activities, prompts, or reflections that you can build into class time, the assignment, or as homework in order to help students draw on, activate, and/or repurpose/adapt their prior knowledge.

As Chapter 4 suggested, students also bring with them prior knowledge and experience that is cultural and personal. Sometimes, this can lead to troublesome experiences learning new threshold concepts or even more basic course material that is simply unfamiliar or at odds with their personal experiences, values, and home cultures. For example, Elizabeth and her former student, Nicolette Clement, wrote about Nicolette's experiences as a first-generation college student from a conservative working-class family encountering new and challenging ideas about gender, sexuality, and art in an honors seminar course (Wardle & Clement, 2017). Nicolette's prior experiences and family values were at odds with the course content, and because her instructors did not provide space for her to reflect on the conflicts, she struggled to speak and write about the course material. Her writing illustrated these moments of conflict, but because her teachers were not aware of the conflicts, they attributed her writing challenges to lack of understanding or preparation. Other researchers also identified instances where students' prior knowledge led to what was perceived as "problematic" readings but, upon investigation, proved to be related to the lenses that came from their proior experiences (Hull & Rose, 1990; Sternglass, 1997).

In situations like these, writing can serve as an opportunity for students to reflect (for no grade, and perhaps not even to be shared with the teacher) about how the current course material aligns or conflicts with their values and cultural experiences. While humanities and social science courses may frequently attend to topics that can conflict with students' values and home cultures, science courses may also do this (consider, for example, topics such as evolution or vaccines). And all courses use some research methods and data/evidence and do not allow for others (for example, narrative and personal experience may not be allowed at all in science or engineering courses and may need to be front and center in some humanities courses), which may prove difficult for some students. Building in opportunities to reflect on what is being asked of students and how they are able to bring their prior knowledge, values, and experiences to bear is an important opportunity to engage all students, Chapter 4 illustrated.

Activity 5.10: Identifying and Working with Conflicts of Culture or Values

1. Consider some of the ideas, topics, and content of your courses that at times cause students to feel conflicts with their existing values and home cultures. What are they and why have they caused conflicts (if you know)?
2. Next, identify a few points in those courses when you could invite students to reflect on the conflicts they may be experiencing in a safe way. For example, invite them to freewrite for a few minutes in class about the conflicts or invite them to engage in small group discussions about conflicts that students might experience when they engage with these ideas.
3. Finally, consider how you will invite students to integrate their reflections on possible conflicts into the coursework. For example, if they know that discussions of evolution conflict with the beliefs of their religious communities, what strategies can you invite them to use in order to engage with the material of the course?

Some strategies for helping students reflect on, activate, and effectively draw on or use prior knowledge include:

- *Short surveys* (at the beginning of the course, a new unit, or a major assignment) that ask questions such as: what do you know about X? Where have you done Y before? What questions do you have about this content/genre? You might refer to the questions included in Activity 4.3 for this, as well.
- *Brief reflective writing*: ask students to write briefly about the topic or the genre/assignment type: what do they think of/what comes to mind about this? Then ask them to talk in pairs and share what they are bringing to this work. Then as a teacher you can identify where their prior knowledge is useful or correct, where they may need to adjust their ideas, and/or where they may need to repurpose or expand their ideas.
- *Group concept review:* Discuss a concept or genre you think students have encountered elsewhere. Ask them to share where they have encountered it, and then illustrate how they will be using/encountering the concept in your class/field/profession.
- *Reflect and Expect chart:* Ask students to identify what they already know about a concept or genre, what they want to know, what they have already learned about it, and what they want/expect to learn.

In all cases, activities to help students reflect on and activate prior knowledge should be very low stakes: the goal is not to grade these but to use them as scaffolding to help students usefully engage in the work of your course(s). It is also helpful to use these activities throughout the course, whenever new content or genres are introduced, not just at the beginning of the course, even connecting new ideas in the course to material you previously covered in the course.

Roles for Writing in Supported Learning Environments

As you have seen while engaging in the activities of this book, there are many uses for writing within a course. It is important when designing a course to clarify your own goals at different points and ensure that you are using writing—and grading (or not grading) writing—in ways that align with your goals. It's helpful to think about why you're asking students to write at particular times in the course. For instance, writing can be used:

- To support student learning and reflection. Small writing activities (as the previous section illustrated) can be used for a variety of purposes: for instance, for students to work with difficult concepts, reflect on their prior knowledge or performance, or serve as components of larger projects. These kinds of activities most frequently fall under the "writing to learn" umbrella.
- As a means of communication and conversation. As Chapter 2 discussed, writers often write to communicate with others—to share their ideas, to get feedback, to connect. In courses, writing is often implemented as a strategy for students to share their ideas with a teacher or with other students. Research, too, is often referred to as a process of dialogue with others, a way of "entering the conversation" (Rose, 1989). Often, when writing is used as a form of conversation with other sources (as in research-based writing) there are expectations about how those other sources or voices will be incorporated. The discussion of source use and citational study in Chapter 3 is important to consider here, since the quality of the writing may depend on the extent to which students successfully conform to citational or stylistic expectations. In these instances, "learning to write" activities—that is, opportunities for students to practice and receive feedback on the conventions of the genre and disciplinary style—are important.
- As a tool for assessment. Writing can also show you what students know and have learned or what they are able to do.

As you introduce writing, it's key to clarify the goals and uses of those writing tasks—for yourself and for students. Different goals lead to different choices about feedback, as well, as delineated in the following chart. You can read much more about these choices in books like *Ungrading: Why Rating Students Undermines Learning (and What to Do Instead)* (Blum, 2020), or *Specifications Grading: Restoring Rigor, Motivating Students, and Saving Faculty Time* (Nilson, 2015), or blogs like "Grading for Growth" (https://gradingforgrowth.com, Grading for Growth, n.d.).

Table 5.2. Writing Goals

Goal	Feedback	Grading
Reflection	Encouragement for next steps	Completion or ungraded
Writing to learn complicated ideas, concepts, or theories	Definition—correct and fully developed? Application—appropriate and fully explained?	Completion or small percentage of total grade
Communication/conversation	Evidence/data appropriate? Evidence/data incorporated in ways expected by readers in the field?	Completion or small percentage of total grade
Assessment—showing what's known/been learned about X	How/did the writing show what the writer was expected to? Where did the writing need further development to do so? What ideas in the writing were appropriate/accurate? Where could the writer improve knowledge of ideas in the writing?	Provided previously scaffolded (through lower-stakes writing); higher percentage of total grade, potentially rubric with comments

Activity 5.11: Identifying Purposes for Writing in Your Course

Review the writing assignments or activity in the course you're focusing on. Using terms from chart above (and potentially adding to or modifying it), identify the purposes for each of your assignments or activities. After you've identified the purposes, make notes for yourself about what text the student should or would produce related to that purpose. Note that if you identify multiple purposes, you might want to revise so that each writing activity has one purpose, or one primary purpose.

The Importance of Modeling

As you work with students to practice with and then use genres of writing in your field, students will be more successful if you provide them with models of what you expect, as well as opportunities to study and practice with elements of those models that you think are especially important. Chapters 2 and 3 provided you with many examples of how to study writing and writing practices, and then consider the implications for your teaching. You can engage in that study with students in your field as well. First, you'll need to determine what you want them to know. For example: how arguments are structured, what different elements of writing (abstracts, thesis statements, evidence/data from others, citations) look like, what stylistic conventions are expected (sentence length, syntax, or mechanics)? Whatever you want students to focus on, if you can spend time (even a single class day) providing them an opportunity to focus explicitly on the *structure, syntax, citations, and other genre conventions* of a model, they will have a much clearer idea of how to compose the texts you expect.

Vanessa Woods, a faculty member in psychological and brain sciences, for instance, found that students struggled with one of the starting points for a research-based analysis in her psychology methods course. To help them get going, Woods created a starting model with component elements for her students to write the results of an ANOVA as part of a peer review activity (see ANOVA Write-Up in the appendix for this chapter).[5] Students then build on this model in the broader research assignment that they produce. Woods tells students that this is a "bare minimum" starting point, and they should plan on making the writing seem less repetitive and more expansive.

A 2 (___) x 2 (____) ANOVA was conducted and showed that IV1 on the DV was [significant/insignificant] (F[df, df] = ____ p = ____), (Ms = ____ and ____). [make sure to indicate what each mean is referring to). This indicates that the main effect of [IV1] on [DV] was [explain in words]. The IV2 on the DV was [also insignificant/insignificant] (F[df, df] = ____ p = ____), (Ms = ____ and ____). [make sure to indicate what each mean is referring to). This indicates that the main effect of [Moderator] on [DV] was [significant/not significant]. This indicates the main effect of [Moderator] on [DV] was [explain in words]. The interaction effect of [IV1] and [IV2/Moderator] on [DV] was [insignificant/insignificant] (F[df, df] = ____ p = ____) [compare cell means here] This indicates that there is an interaction between [IV1] and [Moderator] on [DV] [explain in words].

Another example comes from gerontologists and philosophers at Miami University, who annotated pieces of writing to show students examples of the kinds of textual "moves" they are expected to make. See https://tinyurl.com/6aycxbjk and https://tinyurl.com/y6rz4ppa, respectively.

---

5. In addition to linking directly to resources on the web, we provide archived versions of the materials in the appendix on this book's web page at https://wac.colostate.edu/books/practice/expertise.

Activity 5.12: Using Models to Reinforce "Good Writing"

Find the best model of the kind of writing you'd like students to produce to demonstrate knowledge in the class you're focusing on in this chapter. This could be a short answer on a multiple choice exam, an extended research project, or anything else.

After you've located the model, focus on one to two elements of writing that you consider *especially important* for students to do correctly in the writing. Write for yourself: What makes this an especially excellent example? You'll want to write as many sentences describing the good/outstanding qualities of the writing as you can. Consider: is it the way the analysis is outlined? Is it the use of evidence? Connections between the writer's thinking and the data? The use of a theoretical framework? The seamless ways they have incorporated evidence?

Note that it is highly unlikely that one of the outstanding qualities you will define is the elegant use of commas or periods. That's because readers notice mechanics and punctuation only when they violate our expectations and start to pull us away from what they *do* care about in writing. This is a distinction worth considering when you work with students. A perfectly punctuated paper that says nothing is not a good paper. On the other hand, a paper whose *unintentional violation* of expectations of mechanics or punctuation that refocuses readers' attention on those features may become distracting.

Feedback

As you design your course and build activities and assignments, you will want to consider how particular tasks contribute to students' knowledge and who can provide feedback on them. It would be easy to make every activity and task one that was seen and responded to by you as the instructor; however, that is neither practical nor in keeping with what scholars know about how learning works. As previous chapters demonstrated, learning and writing are social. Thus, designing a course in which students also learn together, try out new ideas with one another, give feedback on ideas, and work together is most effective in helping students reach the learning goals you have set. Students can also engage in self-reflection. When feedback from you as the instructor is necessary, there are many ways to provide such feedback beyond line-editing each student's work (which is, in fact, not as helpful to their learning as many faculty believe it to be).

Self-Reflection

In smaller classes, you can provide students with structured prompts asking about how they went about the writing, what they included and chose not to include, and what more they think is important. Even in large STEM courses students often complete exam wrappers, such as the exam wrapper found in the appendix for this chapter, that serve the same function. With guided prompts from you, students can look at their own work with fresh eyes and then revise.

Peer Feedback

Whether face-to-face or via electronic platforms (such as ones built into Canvas or other LMSs, or external platforms like Eli Review, at https://elireview.com), students can provide feedback on one another's writing. It's useful to remember that providing feedback is something people have to learn to do well; it doesn't come naturally. Faculty are often disappointed when peer review isn't useful. But peer review can be incredibly helpful when it is highly structured—when it focuses on specific elements of writing, and when students receive specific prompts both for the writing and review activities. For instance, you might consider developing separate peer review activities focusing on *concepts* that you want students to work with, and *ways of writing* that they should use for those concepts. This is what instructors like Woods have done. The ANOVA model discussed at the beginning of this session is part of a peer review assignment where students read one another's ANOVA descriptions and provide feedback to peers where they reflect the expected elements, where they need revision, and what they can to improve the *way of writing* that is expected in psychological and brain sciences papers.

Alternatively, in an international relations course, political scientist Julia Morse wants to make sure that students understand and can apply paradigms that "international relations scholars employ to make sense of a chaotic world and explain state behavior." In a peer review activity, then, she asks students to "write a summary of each of the four IR paradigms that . . . describe[s] the core motivating assumptions of the paradigm,"and then to "practice writing a thesis statement for each paragraph" that explains "how that paradigm expects states to behave in the international system." She reminds students that "Each thesis statement is about implications. Ask yourself: If the assumptions of this paradigm are true, what does that mean for state behavior and the international system?" She then provides an example to students, and explains why they are practicing writing about these concepts. Morse's peer review opens by reminding students that "as a reviewer, your job is to help classmates understand the nuances of the different IR theories," and that reviewing responses will also "strengthen your [own] understanding of each theory's core" as they prepare to write their first answer. They then: 1) indicate, via a trait ID checklist, whether the definitions of each IR theory include the relevant elements; 2) indicate how strong the response's "grasp" of the theories seem to be on a 3-point scale; 3) explain why they rated the "grasp" as they did and indicate, as a reader, what more they'd like to know; and 4) provide any final feedback. Both the prompts for the writing and peer review activity are created and delivered in Eli Review, an online peer review platform. They are highly structured, providing students guidance so that they can practice with the difficult ideas in the course, and provide useful feedback for their peers.

The models of peer review provided by Woods and Morse are among hundreds developed by instructors that incorporate the "highly structured" approach. Early studies of this approach to peer feedback in a STEM course show that when students complete two or more writing and review activities during a term, they earn higher grades. This finding controls for previous STEM GPA, as well as demographic factors (Woods et al., 2021). It's also worth considering the timing of peer review, too. You can do so by asking yourself how and when, in your life as a writer, you relied on others for different types of feedback. Sometimes conversations before beginning to write are the most effective use of peer feedback. Other times, you may have a complete but very rough draft and seek guidance on big ideas rather than editing. Help students engage in peer interaction around writing all stages of that writing, and to ask specifically for the kind of feedback they need at that point.

Teacher Feedback

When most students think of feedback, of course they focus on feedback from instructors. As you think about the balance between peer and instructor (or TA) feedback, it's also worth considering when in the process of writing students benefit the most from extended feedback from you. However, feedback needs to happen at the right time and be followed by the opportunity to act on the feedback (Ambrose et al., 2010). Faculty often invest effort in end-of-course or end-of-project comments which students are unlikely to read or act on; it can be more productive for student learning for faculty to instead invest that labor to feedback earlier in the course or earlier in the project when students can actively read and use those comments to guide revision.

As you comment, it might be useful to remind yourself: if a writer knew how to do the thing you were asking them to do in an assignment, they would do it. No student sits down to write with the intention of frustrating the person commenting on or grading their assignment—and yet, often instructors approach feedback with frustration. Comments that tell students "wrong word," or "not this," or "evidence!" don't help writers do a better job, either—because, again, if writers knew what something was supposed to look like or contain, they would produce writing that looked like what was expected. As you consider assigning and providing feedback, then, consider the following strategies:

- Chunk major assignments into smaller components or assign draft due dates. This allows opportunities for feedback on drafts or pieces of a draft before a student gets too far down the road on a large project.

- Concentrate on a few things at a time based on priorities. Few writers are able to write a complete, comprehensive, insightful, appropriately-sourced document that uses appropriate mechanics (syntax) and punctuation. Instead, as you've learned by reflecting on your own processes, writers work in their own chunks. When you give feedback, work in the same way. It's typical to focus on *higher order* concerns first, like research questions, claims, lines of argument, evidence, and organization. Once those are in place, focus on *lower order* concerns like syntax and punctuation. After all: a perfectly punctuated paper that says nothing isn't going to be very good.

- Focus your feedback on a few areas at a time. Research has clearly shown that too much feedback tends to overwhelm students. They can't be sure what to do first (or second, or third), and it's challenging to identify what's most important. It's likely, too, that students will focus on what's easiest—often, mechanical errors or punctuation—rather than higher-order concerns (Ambrose et al., 2010; Sommers, 1982).

- Identify patterns. Research shows that when it comes to lower-order concerns, people make errors in patterns (Shaughnessy, 1977). For example, they might not use commas or periods in ways deemed appropriate for the genre, resulting in run-on sentences or comma splices. When you see patterns, don't "fix" them. Writers can work on these patterns most effectively when commenters point to them and show how to address them (Ambrose et al., 2010; Shaughnessy, 1977).

- Don't write over students' words. Remember that students need to do the writing—it's not helpful when you do it for them, and writing over another person's language is a form of taking over ownership of the text.

After you have given students feedback and they have engaged in further drafting and revision, they will need additional feedback from you on how effectively they addressed the concerns or suggestions. Ask students to read your feedback and actively make a plan to respond to it. For example, you can give them a few minutes in class to read or listen to feedback, ask clarifying questions about what you mean, and write a revision plan for their own use (describing what they will draft and revise next and when). This is useful even at the end of a major writing task, when students can reflect on how to transfer what they have learned to future writing tasks.

While the idea of giving feedback to all students on drafts might feel overwhelming, it need not be. Many instructors have felt quite liberated after they've realized that they don't need to line edit and can focus their feedback and have students conduct productive peer review even before handing in writing for instructor or TA commentary. When you do provide feedback, you can do so when it's most useful for writers to apply your commentary. You also do not have to respond to each student individually. Instead, for example, you might read all the students' research questions and then give oral feedback to the entire class about how to improve the questions—and then provide a few minutes in class for students to engage in this revision and share their new question with a partner. You might provide models of what you are asking them to write (for example, models of a methods section) and then after reading their drafts, return to the models with the full class to illustrate some rhetorical moves that the models made that students could better emulate.

If you do give individual feedback, you don't necessarily need to do so with written comments. You might consider recording oral comments using a program like Screencast-o-matic or Jing so that you can show areas you want students to attend to while orally walking them through your feedback.

Many instructors like to use rubrics in order to cut down on response time. If you do use rubrics, consider why and when. If you have been providing feedback throughout the drafting process using shared criteria that all the students have been engaged with all along, then a rubric might serve as a final opportunity to give quick feedback on how the draft has improved. Many rubrics are generic and acontextual, however, and thus not particularly useful as a feedback mechanism (Anson et al., 2012). Just rating "correctness, clarity, evidence," for example, is not very useful (for reasons named repeatedly throughout this book).

Keep in mind that grades are not equivalent to feedback. Grades may provide an overall sense of how close the student is to the target you have in mind, but grades do not convey what has gone well or badly and what students might do to continue to improve. Thus, grades are summative, end of project or end of course assessments. If the goal is improved learning, however, students need *feedback* (Ambrose et al., 2010).

As you provide students with feedback, try to respond with compassion and with a focus on learning. Students are learners who will not improve overnight; all of us always have more to learn about writing. As students write their way into your field or profession, they need opportunities to practice and receive feedback across time (in your class and in other classes). Keep your expectations for improvement in line with what you have learned in this book about how learning and writing work—and remember your own experience learning to write in new and difficult ways.

Preframing, linking performance and prior learning, providing constructive feedback, defining terms, scaffolding writing—these are all elements of providing students access to what makes writing good in your discipline or field. This is the epitome of "learning to write." At the same time, students can "write to learn," using writing to study and practice with those characteristics. The activities in this chapter will enact WTL and LTW manageably, in ways that make your teaching (and perhaps that of TAs, if applicable) more efficient, effective, and enjoyable. At the same time, the activities in this chapter are integrally linked to all that you've explored in previous chapters: defining core (threshold) concepts, learning bottlenecks, or ways of thinking and practicing in your field, identifying genres and conventions, and learning about learners. This is because writing is always linked to individual identities and disciplinary/field membership that need to be carefully yoked.

Activity 5.13 Linking Performance and Prior Learning

Potentially focusing on the same piece/element of writing you did in classroom application Activity 5.9, reflect on where students sometimes struggle with the writing—for instance, with defining concepts or theories and applying them; with incorporating evidence; or something else.

Once you have defined these elements, write down:

1. What the element of writing that students have struggled *should* look like (i.e., how to do what you're asking);
2. Why it should look the way it does (i.e., what it does for the field, why it has been deemed important to write it in this way, why the concept is important for the field);
3. Why it is important in this class to revise the writing as you've outlined.

This explanation, initially written for you, can serve as the foundation for framing you can give to students ("It's important to emphasize this in your writing because _____"; or "The citations are structured as they are because _____") and/or feedback that you provide.

Conclusion

We opened this book with the idea that writing is never "just writing." We said then and reiterate now that writing is simultaneously a means for people to learn, an expression of personal identity, and a way of signaling belonging. As writing instructors and program leaders ourselves, we have frequently been asked by faculty in other departments to provide "quick tips" that they can use to engage students in writing. But over the decades that the two of us have taught writing and worked with faculty to do the same, we've come to develop a framework and series of activities that help faculty fully explore their knowledge and their disciplinary communities of practice, then build writing activities that provide access and opportunity for students in those communities. This book represents those activities in written form, underscored by research and illustrated by the pedagogical activities of the many colleagues with whom we have worked over the years.

As you move forward to build your courses after working through the ideas in this book, we urge you to think about writing as the top level of a very deep well. That's because often, writers look to writing as a strategy for learning and knowing (writing to learn, what you might think of as digging out the hole for the well), as well as a strategy for showing what they've learned (capping the well). This enables *access* to your field or discipline, providing students with ways to look at and practice with how knowledge is constructed there. But solely focusing on access overlooks the ways that accepted forms of constructed knowledge have been reified through the perspectives of those who are already disciplinary or field insiders. That's why we've also asked you to consider where to provide *opportunity* as well, learning more about the identities and commitments of the writers with whom you're working and making space for them in your courses.

The totality of this book—its chapters, reflective and classroom activities, the appendices, and even the research that underscores it—reflects the three commitments: 1) *teaching with writing* (writing to learn), 2) *teaching writing* (teaching students conventions or expectations of disciplinary genres), and 3) *teaching writers* (focusing on the writers in your classes). As we close this book, we invite you to bring together in one location the ideas you've developed as you've read the book in a single location, and consider the following questions:

1. How can you *use writing* as a means of explicitly considering the epistemologies in your discipline or field?
2. How can you *teach with writing*, helping writers learn about and practice with knowledge in your courses and field? What activities can help students see how knowledge is built through the conventions of written communication, and what activities will help them draw on that knowledge for their own writing?

3. How can you *teach writing*, providing opportunities for students to practice with conventions of knowledge-creating in your discipline, and
   understand how and why they are constructed as they are?

Teaching writing and teaching with writing are necessary for providing students *access* to your discipline or your course. The fourth question focuses on
opportunity:

4. How will you *teach writers* in the course? What strategies from this book
   can help you develop empathetic knowledge, then design activities in
   your course or assignment to tap into their identities, commitments, and
   knowledges? When our teaching and research loads are high, it is easy
   to overlook this piece. However, because literacy and identity are co-
   constitutive (Descourtis et al., 2019), and embodied (Krzus-Shaw, 2019).
   Thus, if we want to invite students into our work, we must provide them
   opportunities to participate, not just regurgitate. Your students must find
   meaningful connections between the course material and their own priorities and interests.

Because writing—and teaching—and all forms of knowledge-making are
social, we encourage you to invite your colleagues into the work of this book.
Consider forming reading groups or learning communities, and working with
your colleagues to think through courses, programs, majors, and high-stakes
exams. Together, you can innovate deep learning experiences for your students,
and enrich your field.

References

Addy, T. M., Dube, D., Mitchell, K. A. & SoRelle, M. E. (2021). *What inclusive instructors do: Principles and practices for excellence in college teaching.* Stylus Publishing.

Adler-Kassner, L. (2017). Chair's address: Because writing is never just writing. *College Composition and Communication, 69*(2), 317–340.

Adler-Kassner, L. (2019). Designing for "more": Writing's knowledge and epistemologically inclusive teaching. *The WAC Journal, 30,* 35–63.

Adler-Kassner, L. & Majewski, J. (2015). Extending the invitation: Threshold concepts, professional development, and outreach. In L. Adler-Kassner & E. Wardle (Eds.), *Naming what we know: Threshold concepts of writing studies* (pp. 186–202). Utah State University Press.

Adler-Kassner, L. & Wardle, E. (2015). *Naming what we know: Threshold concepts of writing studies.* Utah State University Press.

Agnew, E. & McLaughlin, M. (2001). Those crazy gates and how they swing: Tracking the system that tracks African-American students. In G. McNenny & S. H. Fitzgerald (Eds.), *Mainstreaming basic writers: Politics and pedagogies of access* (pp. 85–100). Routledge.

Ahmed, S. K. (2018). *Being the change: Lessons and strategies to teach social comprehension.* Heinemann.

Ambrose, S. A., Bridges, M. W., DiPietro M., Lovett, M. C. & Norman, M. K. (2010). *How learning works: Seven research-based principles for smart teaching.* Jossey-Bass.

Anson, C. M., Dannels, D. P., Flash, P., Gaffney, A. L. H. (2012). Big rubrics and weird genres: The futility of using generic assessment tools across diverse instructional contexts. *Journal of Writing Assessment, 5*(1), 1–15.

Anson, C. M. & Neely, S. (2010). The army and the academy as textual communities: Exploring mismatches in the concepts of attribution, appropriation, and shared goals. *Kairos: A Journal of Rhetoric, Technology, and Pedagogy, 14*(3). http://kairos .technorhetoric.net/14.3/topoi/anson-neely/index.html.

Ardizzone, T., Breithaupt, F. & Gutjahr, P. C. (2004). Decoding the humanities. *New directions for teaching and learning, 98,* 45–56.

Ardizzone, T., Breithaupt, F. & Gutjahr, P. C. (2004a). Step 1: Identify a bottleneck to learning. http://decodingthedisciplines.org/step–1-identify-a-bottleneck-to -learning/.

Asai, D. (2019). To learn inclusion skills, make it personal. *Nature, 565*(7741), 537. https://doi.org/10.1038/d41586-019-00282-y.

Baillie, C., Bowden, J. A. & Meyer, J. H. F. (2013). Threshold capabilities: Threshold concepts and knowledge capability linked through variation theory. *Higher Education, 65*(2), 227–246.

Baker-Bell, A. (2020). Linguistic justice: Black language, literacy, identity, and pedagogy. Taylor & Francis. https://doi.org/10.4324/9781315147383.

Ball, C. E. & Loewe, D. M. (2017). *Bad ideas about writing*. West Virginia University Libraries.

Bawarshi, A. S. & Reiff, M. J. (2010). *Genre: An introduction to history, theory, research, and pedagogy*. Parlor Press; The WAC Clearinghouse. https://wac.colo state.edu/books/referenceguides/bawarshi-reiff/.

Bazerman, C. (1987). Codifying the social scientific style: The APA Publication Manual as behaviorist rhetoric. In J. S. Nelson, A. Megill & D. N. McCloskey. *The rhetoric of the human sciences: Language and argument in scholarship and public affairs* (pp. 125–144). The University of Wisconsin Press.

Bazerman, C. (2015). Writing speaks to situations through recognizable forms. In L. Adler-Kassner & E. Wardle (Eds.), *Naming what we know: Threshold concepts of writing studies* (pp. 35–37). Utah State University Press.

Bazerman, C. & Prior, P. (2003). *What writing does and how it does it: An Introduction to analyzing texts and textual practices*. Routledge.

Bazerman, C. & Russell, D. R. (2003). *Writing selves, writing societies: Research from activity perspectives*. The WAC Clearinghouse; Mind, Culture, and Activity. https://doi.org/10.37514/PER-B.2003.2317.

Berkenkotter, C., Huckin, T. N. & Ackerman, J. (1988). Conventions, conversations, and the writer: Case study of a student in a rhetoric Ph.D. program. *Research in the Teaching of English, 22*(1), 9–44.

Binning, K. R., Kaufmann, N., McGreevy, E. M., Fotuhi, O., Chen, S., Marshman, E., Kalender, Z. Y., Limeri, L. B., Betancur, L. & Singh, C. (2020). Changing social contexts to foster equity in college science courses: An ecological-belonging intervention. *Psychological Science, 31*(9), 1059–1070. https://doi.org/10.1177/095 6797620929984.

Blum, S. D. (2020). *Ungrading: Why rating students undermines learning (and what to do instead)*. West Virginia University Press.

Bransford, J. D., Brown, A. L. & Cocking, R. R. (2000). *How people learn: Brain, mind, experience, and school*. National Academy Press.

Bransford, J. & Johnson, M. (1972). Contextual prerequisites for understanding: Some investigations of comprehension and recall. *Journal of Verbal Learning and Verbal Behavior 11*, 717–726.

Buranen, L. & Stephenson, D. (2009). Collaborative authorship in the sciences: Anti-ownership and citation practices in chemistry and biology. In C. P. Haviland & J. A. Mullin (Eds.), *Who owns this text? Plagiarism, authorship, and disciplinary cultures* (pp. 49–79). Utah State University Press.

Campelia, G. D. (2017). Empathic knowledge: The import of empathy's social episte-mology. *Social Epistemology, 31*(6), 530–544.

Carter, M. (2007). Ways of knowing, doing, and writing in the disciplines. *College Composition and Communication, 58*(3), 385–418.

Chamany, K., Allen, D. & Tanner, K. (2008). Making biology learning relevant to students: Integrating people, history, and context into college biology teaching. *CBE–Life Sciences Education, 7*(3), 267–278.

Charity Hudley, A., Dickter, C. L. & Franz, H. A. (2022). *Guides for undergraduate research and for college student writers and their instructors*. Students' Right to Their Own Writing: https://charityhudleydickterfranz.com/.

Cohen, G. L., Steele, C. M. & Ross, L. D. (1999). The mentor's dilemma: Providing critical feedback across the racial divide. *Personality and Social Psychology Bulletin, 25*(10), 1302–1318. https://doi.org/10.1177/0146167299258011.

Conference on College Composition and Communication (CCCC). (1974, reaffirmed 2014). Students' right to their own language. https://cccc.ncte.org/cccc/resources/positions/srtolsummary.

Conference on College Composition and Communication (CCCC). (2020). This ain't another statement! This is a DEMAND for Black linguistic justice! https://cccc.ncte.org/cccc/demand-for-black-linguistic-justice.

Connors, R. J. (1999). The rhetoric of citation systems–Part II: Competing epistemological values in citation. *Rhetoric Review, 17*(2), 219–245.

D'Angelo, B. J., Jamieson, S., Maid, B. & Walker, J. R. (Eds.). (2016). *Information Literacy: Research and Collaboration across Disciplines.* The WAC Clearinghouse; University Press of Colorado. https://doi.org/10.37514/PER-B.2016.0834.

Davidson, C. N. (2019). Why we need a new higher education: We have a responsibility to the next generation of students. *Liberal Education, 105*(2), 6–13.

Davis, L. P. & Museus, S. D. (2019a, July 19). Identifying and disrupting deficit thinking. National Center for Institutional Diversity. https://medium.com/national-center-for-institutional-diversity/identifying-and-disrupting-deficit-thinking-cbc6da326995 .

Davis, L. P. & Museus, S. D. (2019b). What is deficit thinking? An analysis of conceptualizations of deficit thinking and implications for scholarly research. *Currents, 1*(1). http://dx.doi.org/10.3998/currents.17387731.0001.110.

Desourtis, S., Isaac J., Senanayake, S. & Swift, B. (2019). Literacy and identity are co-constitutive. In L. Adler-Kassner & E. Wardle (Eds.), *(Re)Considering what we know* (pp. 39–40). Utah State University Press.

Decoding the Disciplines. (n.d.). *Improving student learning.* Decoding the Disciplines. https://decodingthedisciplines.org.

Dewsbury, B. M. (2020). Deep teaching in a college STEM classroom. Cultural Studies of Science Education, 15(1), 169–191. https://doi.org/10.1007/s11422-018-9891-z.

Dewsbury, B. & Brame, C. J. (2019). Inclusive teaching. CBE—Life Sciences Education, 18(2), 1–5. https://doi.org/10.1187/cbe.19-01-0021.

Dryer, D. B. (2015). Words get their meaning from other words. In L. Adler-Kassner & E. Wardle (Eds.), *Naming what we know: Threshold concepts of writing studies* (pp. 23–25). Utah State University Press.

Eodice, M., Geller, A. E. & Lerner, N. (2017). *The meaningful writing project: Learning, teaching, and writing in higher education.* Utah State University Press.

Estrem, H. (2015). Writing is a knowledge-making activity. In L. Adler-Kassner & E. Wardle (Eds.), *Naming what we know: Threshold Concepts of writing studies* (pp. 19–20). Utah State University Press.

Flanagan, M. (n.d.). *A short introduction and a bibliography from 2003 to 2018.* Threshold Concepts: Undergraduate Teaching, Postgraduate Training, Professional Development and School Education. https://www.ee.ucl.ac.uk/~mflanaga/thresholds.html.

Foss, S. K. (1989). Rhetorical criticism: Exploration & practice. Waveland Press.

Freire, P. (1970). Pedagogy of the oppressed. The Continuum International Publishing Group.

Gannon, K. M. (2020). Radical hope: A teaching manifesto. West Virginia University Press.

Gick, M. L. & Holyoak, K. J. (1980). Analogical problem solving. Cognitive Psychology, 12(3), 306–355. https://doi.org/10.1016/0010-0285(80)90013-4.

Gonzales, L. (2018). *Sites of translation: What multilinguals can teach us about digital writing and rhetoric*. University of Michigan Press.

Gonzales, L. (2022). *Designing multilingual experiences in technical communication*. Utah State University Press.

González, N., Moll, L. C. & Amanti, C. (2005). *Funds of knowledge: Theorizing practices in households, communities and classrooms*. Routledge.

Grading for Growth. (n.d.). *Grading for growth*. Substack. https://gradingforgrowth.com/.

Hammond, Z. (2014). *Culturally responsive teaching and the brain: Promoting authentic engagement and rigor among culturally and linguistically diverse students*. Sage Publications.

Harrison, C. D., Nguyen, T. A., Seidel, S. B., Escobedo, A. M., Hartman, C., Lam, K., Liang, K. S., Martens, M., Acker, G. N., Akana, S. F., Balukjian, B., Benton, H. P., Blair, J. R., Boaz, S. M., Boyer, K. E., Bram, J. B., Burrus, L. W., Byrd, D. T., Caporale, N., . . . Tanner, K. D. (2019). Investigating instructor talk in novel contexts: Widespread use, unexpected categories, and an emergent sampling strategy. *CBE—Life Sciences Education, 18*(3), ar47, 1–23. https://doi.org/10.1187/cbe.18-10-0215.

Hart-Davidson, B. (2015). Genres are enacted by writers and readers. In L. Adler-Kassner & E. Wardle (Eds.), *Naming what we know: Threshold Concepts of writing studies* (pp. 39–40). Utah State University Press.

hooks, b. (1994). *Teaching to transgress*. Routledge.

Hull, G. & Rose, M. (1990). "This wooden shack place": The logic of an unconventional reading. *College Composition and Communication, 41*(3), 287–298. https://doi.org/10.2307/357656.

Hyland, K. (1999). Academic attribution: Citation and the construction of disciplinary knowledge. *Applied Linguistics, 20*(3), 341–367. http://dx.doi.org/10.1093/applin/20.3.341.

Hyland, K. (2002). Activity and evaluation: Reporting practices in academic writing. In J. Flowerdew (Ed.), *Academic discourse* (pp. 115–130). Routledge.

Hyland, K. (2004). *Disciplinary discourses: Social interactions in academic writing*. University of Michigan Press.

Karatsolis, A. (2016). Rhetorical patterns in citations across disciplines and levels of participation. *Journal of Writing Research, 7*(3), 425–452.

Kim, D. & Olson, W. M. (2020). Using a transfer-focused writing pedagogy to improve undergraduates' lab report writing in gateway engineering laboratory courses. *IEEE Transactions on Professional Communication, 63*(1), 64–84.

Krzus-Shaw, K. (2019). Literacy is embodied. In L. Adler-Kassner & E. Wardle (Eds.), *(Re)Considering what we know* (pp. 43–44). Utah State University Press.

Ladson-Billings, G. (2021). *Culturally relevant pedagogy: Asking a different question*. Teachers College Press.

Lave, J. & Wenger, E. (1991). *Situated learning: Legitimate peripheral participation.* Cambridge University Press.

Lerner, N. (2015). Writing is a way of enacting disciplinarity. In L. Adler-Kassner & E. Wardle (Eds.), *Naming what we know: Threshold concepts of writing studies* (pp. 40–41). Utah State University Press.

Linguistic Society of America (LSA). (2019, May). *LSA statement on race.* Linguistic Society of America. https://www.linguisticsociety.org/content/lsa-statement-race.

Loertscher, J. (2011) Threshold concepts in biochemistry. *Biochemistry and Molecular Biology Education, 39*(1), 56–57.

Lunsford, A. (2015a). Writing addresses, invokes, and/or creates audiences. In L. Adler-Kassner & E. Wardle (Eds.), *Naming what we know: Threshold concepts of writing studies* (pp. 20–21). Utah State University Press.

Lunsford, A. (2015b). Writing is informed by prior experience. In L. Adler-Kassner & E. Wardle (Eds.), *Naming what we know: Threshold concepts of writing studies* (pp. 54–55). Utah State University Press.

Maroko, G. M. (2013). Citation practices in selected science and humanities dissertations; Implications for teaching. *American Journal of Educational Research, 1*(4), 126–136.

Mathew, R. (2014, September 23). Writing as translation: So what are you actually asking me to do? [Video]. YouTube. https://www.youtube.com/watch?v=2SzMW LoR4C8.

Mazur, E. (2009). Farewell, lecture? *Science, 323*(5910), 50–51.

McCarthy, L. P. (1987). A stranger in strange lands: A college student writing across the curriculum. *Research in the Teaching of English, 21*(3), 233–265. http://www.jstor.org/stable/40171114.

McNair, T. B., Bensimon, E. M. & Malcom-Piqueux, L. (2020). *From equity talk equity walk: Expanding practitioner knowledge for racial justice in higher education.* Jossey-Bass.

Meyer, J. H. F. & Land, R. (2003). Threshold concepts and troublesome knowledge: linkages to ways of thinking and practising within the disciplines. In C. Rust (Ed.), *Improving student learning: Theory and practice 10 years on* (pp. 412–424). Oxford Centre for Staff Development.

Meyer, J. H. F. & Land, R. (2006). *Overcoming barriers to student understanding: Threshold concepts and troublesome knowledge.* Routledge.

Middendorf, J. & Pace, D. (2004). Decoding the disciplines: A model for helping students learn disciplinary ways of thinking. *New Directions for Teaching and Learning, 2004*(98), 1–12.

Middendorf, J. & Shopkow, L. (2018). *Overcoming student learning bottlenecks: Decode the critical thinking of your discipline.* Stylus Publishing.

Miyake, A., Kost-Smith, L. E., Finkenstein, N. D., Pollock S. J., Cohen, G. L. & Ito, T. A. (2010). Reducing the gender achievement gap in college science: A classroom study of values affirmation. *Science, 330*(6008). https://doi.org/10.1126/science.1195996.

Muhammad, G. (2020). *Cultivating genius: An equity framework for culturally and historically responsive literacy.* Scholastic.

National Academies of Sciences, Engineering, and Medicine. (2018). *How people learn II: Learners, contexts, and cultures.* The National Academies Press.

Nilson, L. B. (2015). *Specifications grading: Restoring rigor, motivating students, and saving faculty time.* Stylus Publishing.

Pace, D. (2017). *The decoding the disciplines paradigm.* Indiana University Press.

Peeck, J., van den Bosch, A. B. & Kreupeling, W. (1982). Effect of mobilizing prior knowledge on learning from text. *Journal of Educational Psychology, 74*(5), 771–777.

Pekrun, R. & Linnenbrink-Garcia, L. (2012). Academic emotions and student engagement. In S. L. Christenson, A. L. Reschly & C. Wylie (Eds.), *Handbook of research on student engagement* (pp. 259–282). Springer. https://doi.org/10.1007/978-1-4614-2018-7_12.

Perkins, D. N. & Salomon, G. (2012). Knowledge to go: A motivational and dispositional view of transfer. *Educational Psychologist, 47*(3), 248–258.

Petraglia, J. (1995). *Reconceiving writing, rethinking writing instruction.* Lawrence Erlbaum Associates.

Porter, J. E. (1986). Intertextuality and the discourse community. *Rhetoric Review, 5*(1), 34–47.

Reiff, M. J. & Bawarshi, A. (2011). Tracing discursive resources: How students use prior genre knowledge to negotiate new writing contexts in first-year composition. *Written Communication, 28*(3), 312–337.

Roberts-Miller, P. (2019). Windsocks and the epistemological/ontological distinction. https://www.patriciarobertsmiller.com/2019/11/27/windsocks-and-the-epistemological-ontological-distinction/.

Roozen, K. (2015a). Texts get their meaning from other texts. In L. Adler-Kassner & E. Wardle (Eds.), *Naming what we know: Threshold concepts of writing studies* (pp. 44–47). Utah State University Press.

Roozen, K. (2015b). Writing is linked to identity. In L. Adler-Kassner & E. Wardle (Eds.), *Naming what we know: Threshold concepts of writing studies* (pp. 50–52). Utah State University Press.

Roozen, K. (2015c). Writing is a social and rhetorical activity. In L. Adler-Kassner & E. Wardle (Eds.), *Naming what we know: Threshold concepts of writing studies* (pp. 17–18). Utah State University Press.

Rosa, J. & Flores, N. (2017). Unsettling race and language: Toward a raciolinguistic perspective. *Language in Society, 46*(5), 621–647. https://doi.org/10.1017/S0047404517000562.

Rose, M. (1985). The language of exclusion: Writing instruction at the university. *College English, 47*(4), 341–359.

Rose, M. (1989). *Lives on the boundary: The struggles and achievements of America's underprepared.* Penguin Books.

Russell, D. (1995). Activity theory and its implications for writing instruction. In J. Petraglia (Ed.), *Reconceiving writing, rethinking writing instruction* (pp. 51–77). Routledge.

Russell, D. (2015). Writing mediates activity. In L. Adler-Kassner & E. Wardle (Eds.), *Naming what we know: Threshold concepts of writing studies* (pp. 26–27). Utah State University Press.

Scott, T. (2015). Writing enacts and creates identities and ideologies. In L. Adler-Kassner & E. Wardle (Eds.), *Naming what we know: Threshold concepts of writing studies* (pp. 48–50). Utah State University Press.

Seidel, S. B., Reggi, A. L., Schinske, J. N., Burrus, L. W. & Tanner, K. D. (2015). Beyond the biology: A systematic investigation of noncontent instructor talk in an introductory biology course. *CBE—Life Sciences Education, 14*(4), ar43, 1–14. https://doi.org/10.1187/cbe.15-03-0049.

Shaughnessy, M. (1977). *Errors and expectations: A guide for the teacher of basic writing.* Oxford University Press.

Shi, L. (2011). Common knowledge, learning, and citation practices in university writing. *Research in the Teaching of English, 45*(3), 308–334.

Shopkow, L. (2010). What decoding the disciplines can offer threshold concepts. In J. H. F. Meyer, R. Land & C. Baillie (Eds.), *Threshold concepts and transformational learning* (pp. 317–331). Brill.

Shukla, S. Y., Theobald, E. J., Abraham, J. K. & Price, R. M. (2022). Reframing educational outcomes: Moving beyond achievement gaps. *CBE–Life Sciences Education, 21*(2), 1–11. https://doi.org/10.1187/cbe.21-05-0130.

Shulman, L. S. (1986). Those who understand: Knowledge growth in teaching. *Educational Researcher, 15*(2), 4–14.

Smitherman, G. (1977). *Talkin and testifyin: The language of Black America.* Houghton Mifflin.

Sommers, N. (1982). Responding to student writing. *College Composition and Communication, 33*(2), 148–156.

Spriggs, W. (2020). Is now a teachable moment for economists? https://www.minneapolisfed.org/~/media/assets/people/william-spriggs/spriggs-letter_0609_b.pdf.

Stassun, K. G., Sturm, S., Holley-Bockelmann, K., Burger, A., Ernst, D. J. & Webb, D. (2011). The Fisk-Vanderbilt Master's-to-Ph.D. Bridge Program: Recognizing, enlisting, and cultivating unrealized or unrecognized potential in underrepresented minority students. *American Journal of Physics, 79*(4), 374–379. https://doi.org/10.1119/1.3546069.

Sternglass, M. S. (1997). *Time to know them: A longitudinal study of writing and learning at the college level.* Routledge.

Swales, J. M. (1990). *Genre analysis: English in academic and research settings.* Cambridge University Press.

UERU. (2020, May 27). *Raising the bar: Equity in online teaching.* [Video]. YouTube. https://www.youtube.com/watch?v=MHT-DYnmbMo.

Villanueva, V. (2015). Writing provides a representation of ideologies and identities In L. Adler-Kassner & E. Wardle (Eds.), *Naming what we know: Threshold concepts of writing studies* (p. 57). Utah State University Press.

Vygotsky, L. S. (Writer), Cole, M., John-Steiner, V., Scribner, S. & Souberman, E. (Eds.). (1978). *Mind in society: The development of higher psychological processes.* Harvard University Press.

Wardle, E. (2009). "Mutt genres" and the goal of FYC: Can we help students write the genres of the university? *College Composition and Communication, 60*(4), 765–789.

Wardle, E. (2017). You can learn to write in general. In C. E. Ball & D. M. Loewe (Eds.), *Bad ideas about writing* (pp. 30–33). West Virginia University Libraries.

Wardle, E. & Clement, N. M. (2017). "The hardest thing with writing is not getting enough instruction": Helping educators guide students through writing challenges. In R. Bass & J. L. Moore (Eds.), *Understanding writing transfer: Implications for transformative student learning in higher education* (pp. 131–143). Stylus Publishing.

Wardle, E., Adler-Kassner, L., Alexander, J., Elliot, N., Hammond, J. W., Poe, M., Rhodes, J. & Womack, A. (2020). Recognizing the limits of threshold concept theory. In L. Adler-Kassner & E. Wardle (Eds.), *(Re)Considering what we know: Learning thresholds in writing, composition, rhetoric, and literacy.* (pp. 15–35). Utah State University Press.

Wenger, E. (1998). *Communities of practice: Learning, meaning, and identity.* Cambridge University Press.

Wiggins, G. & McTighe, J. (1998). *Understanding by design.* Association for Supervision and Curriculum Development.

Williams, J. M. (1981). The phenomenology of error. *College Composition and Communication, 32*(2), 152–168.

Wineburg, S. (2018) *Why learn history when it's already on your phone?* University of Chicago Press.

Woloshyn, V. E., Paivio, A. & Pressley, M. (1994). Use of elaborative interrogation to help students acquire information consistent with prior knowledge and information inconsistent with prior knowledge. *Journal of Educational Psychology, 86*(1), 79–89. https://doi.org/10.1037/0022-0663.86.1.79.

Womack, A. M. (2019). Writing only occurs within accessible conditions. In L. Adler-Kassner & E. Wardle (Eds.), *(Re)Considering what we know: Learning thresholds in writing, composition, rhetoric, and literacy* (pp. 26–29). Utah State University Press.

Woods, V. E., Safronova, M. & Adler-Kassner, L. (2021) Guiding students towards disciplinary knowledge with structured peer review assignments. *Journal of Higher Education Theory and Practice, 21*(4), 160–175. https://doi.org/10.33423/jhetp.v21i4.4216.

Yancey, K. B. (2015). Writers' histories, processes, and identities vary. In L. Adler-Kassner & E. Wardle (Eds.), *Naming what we know: Threshold concepts of writing studies* (pp. 52–54). Utah State University Press.

Yancey, K. B., Robertson, L. & Taczak, K. (2014). *Writing across contexts: Transfer, composition, and sites of writing.* Utah State University Press.

Yosso, T. J. (2005). Whose culture has capital? A critical race theory discussion of community cultural wealth. *Race, Ethnicity and Education, 8*(1), 69–91. https://doi.org/10.1080/1361332052000341006.

Zolan, M., Strome, S. & Innes, R. (2004). Decoding genetics and molecular biology: Sharing the movies in our heads. *New Directions for Teaching and Learning, 2004*(98), 23–32.